July 29,
62

THE CHURCH AT THE END OF THE
FIRST CENTURY

THE CHURCH AT THE END
OF THE FIRST CENTURY

By

G. BARDY

Translated by

P. W. SINGLETON

LONDON

SANDS & CO.

(PUBLISHERS) LIMITED

15 KING STREET, COVENT GARDEN, W.C.2

AND GLASGOW

First published 1938
by Sands & Co. (Publishers) Limited
from 15 King Street, Covent Garden, London, W.C.2
Printed in Great Britain by
Northumberland Press Limited
Gateshead upon Tyne

—

Nihil obstat: GEORGIUS CAN. SMITH, S.Th.D., Ph.D.
Censor deputatus.

Imprimatur: LEONELLUS CAN. EVANS, Vic. Gen.

Westmonasterii, die 6ª Maii 1938.

CONTENTS

CONTENTS

CHAPTER IV

THE JUDAEO-CHRISTIANS AT THE END OF THE
FIRST CENTURY

CHAPTER V

HERESY AT THE END OF THE FIRST CENTURY

CHAPTER VI

CHRISTIANITY AND THE ROMAN EMPIRE AT THE END
OF THE FIRST CENTURY

CHAPTER VII

EXPANSION OF CHRISTIANITY

INTRODUCTION

THE thirty years which passed between the death of Saint Peter and Saint Paul and the death of Saint John were decisive for the Christian Church. One after the other the witnesses of the Saviour's life had disappeared, and the destinies of the work He founded were entrusted to men who had neither known Him, nor seen His miracles, nor received His teaching. The apostles, filled with the grace of the Holy Spirit, had preached with supreme authority; their successors had no other mission than that of guarding and transmitting the deposit they had received from them. Chosen by the Saviour Himself to be His preachers to the ends of the earth, the apostles governed in His name the communities they had founded almost everywhere; their successors ruled the local Churches which were united by the bond of charity and which already turned towards Rome as the centre to which everything must converge.

This period of organization—one would be tempted to write transformation if there was not a danger of the word being misunderstood—was not without its difficulties. Saint Peter and Saint Paul died victims of Nero's persecution. Saint John, according to tradition, was plunged into a cauldron of boiling oil by order of Domitian. From the moment it learnt to know Christianity the Empire condemned it; even Trajan remained faithful on this point to the practice of his predecessors; if he forbade the younger Pliny to seek out Christians, he ordered him to have all those who were denounced and convicted, put to death.

Persecuted by the civil power, the Church had to fight

also against enemies from within. Certain of her children tried to keep her in the bondage of the Mosaic Law, from which she had been liberated by Saint Paul. The capture of Jerusalem by the Romans was certainly a hard blow to Judaic-Christianity, but it did not ruin it, and for a long time a harsh controversy was continued in which the whole of the Old Testament was concerned.

More dangerous were the heresies connected with the Gnostic tendency. The final letters of Saint Paul already inform us of the first manifestation of this movement, which developed especially in Asia Minor, but which was equally troublesome in Egypt and Syria. Throughout the East the religious aspirations of the multitude were seeking a support, and this they thought they had found in the mystery religions which had more or less coalesced into a vast syncretism. Would Christianity accept the alliance that was offered to it? Would it also become an initiation and a gnosis at the risk of corrupting the purity of the deposit confided to it by its divine founder? At any rate the conflict had begun, and we hear its powerful echoes ringing from various points.

Against all these dangers the Church concentrated its forces. At the head of each community, the bishop, heir and successor of the apostles, appears as the leader whose authority all the faithful must recognize. Saint Ignatius of Antioch brings out clearly the unity of the Church which is manifested in the unity of the bishop; but his way of speaking shows definitely that this organization is already traditional and that the origins of the episcopate must be sought long before the first years of the second century.

A formula, at once simple and complete, expressed what was essential in the Christian faith; no one was admitted into the Church unless he accepted all its terms. Later legends attributed the composition of this venerable formula to the apostles themselves. Although in reality the apostles took no part in it, and although the text is not earlier than the second century, nevertheless the Apostles'

Creed does express the faith of the primitive Church; it is the witness of its most ancient beliefs.

The liturgy also was in process of fixation. It is hardly probable, in spite of what has been said, that we still possess the apostolic anaphora, and for a long time the various communities left the duty of expressing their feelings of adoration and gratitude, or of formulating their prayers, to their leaders. But, from the beginning, the Christian life was organized round two essential rites: that of initiation conferred by baptism in the name of the Father and of the Son and of the Holy Spirit; that of the Eucharist celebrated by repeating the Lord's formulae: This is my body; this is the chalice of the new alliance in my blood. The secondary forms of administration varied according to places and periods, while what was essential remained. Saint Paul had already said that there is only one faith and one baptism; Saint Ignatius adds that there is only one bishop and one Eucharist.

We should like to be able to relate the history of these fruitful years as it was unfolded from day to day. But that is a dream to be renounced almost before it is expressed. No one of those who lived at that time troubled himself to edit the annals of the Christian Church for the use of the generations to come. Those who did write, like the apostle Saint John, recalled the great memories of the past as in his Gospel, or, as in the Apocalypse, lifted the veil of the mysterious future. More frequently they composed instructions of the practical order, addressed letters to distant communities and absent friends, preached homilies whose essential traits they afterwards wrote down. These are chance works, without any pretence to literary style, and without any concern for the instruction of the faithful in the future centuries.

A considerable part of these first Christian writings has completely disappeared, and some of them have only been recovered in our days after several centuries of oblivion. Their apostolic origin, their sacred character have naturally preserved from destruction the works of Saint John over which the Church has never ceased to watch. The letter of Saint Clement of Rome, from having been several times copied at the end of the New Testament, has similarly survived all storms. But who will explain by what chances the *Doctrine of the Apostles* was discovered in 1875 in a manuscript of Constantinople, and why the *Odes of Solomon* were recovered in 1909 in a Syriac manuscript from the neighbourhood of the Tigris?

The future may perhaps reserve other surprises of this kind. But we must not rely too much on that; at the most we shall never have sufficient information for the history of the Christian Church at the end of the apostolic period to be related in detail. The importance of the period is, however, so great that already many have attempted to describe it. Coming after so many others we cannot claim originality. We shall try to be clear and to bring out the greatness of the work accomplished by the Christian Church between the years 70–110. May this little book augment in its readers a filial trust in that Mother Church founded by Jesus Christ and nourished by the blood of the apostles.

CHAPTER I

THE WRITINGS

Papias. Hegesippus. The Presbyters. I. The Johannine Writings: The Apocalypse. The Gospel. The Epistles. II. The letter of Saint Clement. III. The letters of Saint Ignatius. IV. The letter of Saint Polycarp. V. The doctrine of the Apostles. VI. The letter of Barnabus. VII. The Apocryphal Gospels: The Gospel according to the Hebrews. The Gospel according to the Egyptians. The Gospel according to Peter. VIII. The Odes of Solomon.

OUR first task is to review the testimonies at our disposal. These testimonies, as we shall see, are not very numerous, but they are almost all contemporary with the events they relate or to which they allude. At the beginning of the fourth century Eusebius of Caesarea certainly possessed a richer and more complete collection than that which has come down to us; through him we also know certain fragments of the most ancient Christian writers; but these are so minute that we learn almost nothing from them.

PAPIAS

What would we not give, however, to have the complete text of the five books of *Exegesis of the Discourses of the Lord*, drawn up before 150 by Papias of Hierapolis? Eusebius has reproduced the prologue to this work: " I will not hesitate to communicate to you, by adding them to my interpretations, all the things I learnt well from the ancients and that I have kept well in my memory, making myself responsible for their truth. For unlike most men,

5

I do not care for those who speak much, but for those who teach the truth; nor for those who recall strange precepts, but for those who recall the precepts given by the Lord to be believed and coming from the truth itself. And if by chance there came one who had frequented the ancients I questioned him about the discourses of the ancients; what had Andrew, Peter, Philip said?   What had Thomas or James said?   What had John or Matthew or some other disciple of the Lord said?   And what do Aristion and John the elder, the disciples of the Lord say?   For I do not think that the contents of books can render me as much service as that which comes from the living personal voice."[1]

We gather from that that Papias took pleasure in questioning the immediate disciples of the Lord or at least those who had come in contact with them, and that he put down their answers in writing.   He must have learnt many interesting details about the period of which we are treating.   Apart from some fragments quoted by Irenaeus and Eusebius the *Exegesis* is lost.   There is some consolation in the fact that the accounts, reproduced by Irenaeus and by Eusebius, of the death of Judas or of the marvellous fertility of the earth during the millennium do not indicate much critical acumen; and, in fact, Eusebius himself asserts that the good bishop was of very limited understanding.

HEGESIPPUS

The *Memoirs or Commentaries* of Hegesippus would doubtless be more interesting and more useful. A Christian of Jewish origin, Hegesippus wrote this work before 180; he concerned himself with establishing the apostolic succession of the different Churches in order to show where and how the true faith was conserved; he declared that " the Church had remained pure and incorruptible up to his own time; those who attempted to corrupt the sound rule of the preaching of redemption had up to then hidden

---

[1] Eusebius, H.E. iii. 29, 3 sq.

themselves in an uncertain shadow. But when the sacred choir of the apostles had come, by different ways, to the end of its life, and when that generation which had had the privilege of hearing the divine wisdom with its own ears had disappeared, then the development of impious error began through the astuteness of false doctors, who, seeing that none of the apostles still lived, thenceforward undertook openly to oppose the teaching of the gnosis, falsely so called, to the preaching of truth."[1]

Since he had lived for a long time in Palestine, Hegesippus was particularly interested in the Christian communities of his native land. Eusebius has preserved certain fragments which refer to the death of James, the brother of the Lord, to his successor in the episcopate, Simeon, son of Clopas and cousin of the Lord, to the measures taken by Vespasian after the capture of Jerusalem against the descendants of David, to the appearance of the last descendants of Jude, the brother of the Lord, before Domitian. He tells us also that Hegesippus " made certain quotations from the Gospel of the Hebrews and from the Syriac Gospel, and especially from the Hebrew dialect, thus showing that he was a believer who had come from the Hebrews, and that he related many things which belonged —though they had not been written down—to the Jewish tradition ".[2] To-day we know very little of the Judaeo-Christians, and the too rare testimonies which give us information about them have sometimes lent themselves to divergent interpretations. Hegesippus' book would be particularly precious in enlightening our ignorance on this point.

THE PRESBYTERS

From certain ecclesiastical writers, and especially from Saint Irenaeus and Clement of Alexandria, we learn also of various traditions attributed to the presbyters. These

[1] Eusebius, H.E. iii. 32.
[2] Eusebius, H.E. iv. 22.

traditions are not of equal value or of equal interest. Some of them are purely doctrinal; others, although of an historical nature, are insignificant. But we also find among them some admirable accounts, such as the one transmitted by Clement of the pardon granted by the apostle Saint John to one of his young disciples who had become the leader of a band of brigands. Such finds are rare, but they show us the value of the old traditions.

All this does not lead us very far; and, in fact, it is to certain works written during the last years of the first century or at the beginning of the second century that we owe the best of our information.

I. THE JOHANNINE WRITINGS

The writings of the apostle Saint John—the Apocalypse, the Gospel and the three Catholic epistles—must be given a place apart. The Church regards these books as inspired; consequently she asks us to treat them with all the respect due to the Word of God. Even if we envisage them here as historical documents, we shall not forget their sacred character.

According to the tradition, John, whom the Saviour had chosen in his early youth, had survived his brethren in the apostolate. It is useless to stop to discuss here an obscure text, attributed to Papias, which has been asserted to contain the proof of John's death at the hands of the Jews before A.D. 50. Actually, the disciple whom Jesus loved had established himself in Asia at a date which cannot be precisely determined, and he had announced the good news of the Saviour in that vast region, where Saint Paul had previously stayed so long.

In the reign of Domitian, for some unknown reason, John was torn from his labours and exiled to the island of Patmos, having first undergone before the Latin Gate the torture of the boiling oil. It was then that he received the revelation related in the Apocalypse, and sent by him to the Seven Churches of Ephesus, Smyrna, Pergamos, Thyatira, Sardis, Philadelphia and Laodicea.

THE APOCALYPSE

The Apocalypse is a strange and mysterious book; the Christian generations have never ceased to read it and to meditate on it, but it is doubtful whether any of them have grasped its entire meaning. The literary genus to which it belongs was then the fashion; the book of Enoch, the book of Jubilees, the testament of the twelve patriarchs at the time of the Maccabees; the Psalms of Solomon under Pompey; the book of the secrets of Enoch, the Assumption of Moses, the third of the Sybilline books, at the beginning of the Christian era, had obtained a brilliant success in Jewish circles. It was natural that Christianity should have its apocalypse also. Men have never ceased to be tremendously interested in the future and to try to penetrate its secret. Instinctively they give as good a welcome to the soothsayer as to the prophet; most often they do not even try to distinguish the one from the other.

John was a prophet; what he wrote were " the faithful and true sayings, and the Lord, the God of the spirits of the prophets, had sent his angel to show his servants the things which must shortly be done ".[1] He had received the mission of delivering the message of hope to his contemporaries, and especially to the faithful of the Seven Churches of Asia. The times were troubled; persecution had begun and threatened to become more acute as time went on. Fear penetrated the hearts of men all the more easily because heresy and immorality had already weakened those communities which had seemed most stable. " To enable the faithful to unmask successfully the wiles of the demon, it was necessary to forearm them against the entice-

[1] Apoc. xxii, 6.

ments which the Beast would use in his perpetual conflict with God. These warnings, in some ways necessarily frightening, were counterbalanced by a clear and precise vision of ultimate victory. This made the faith of the Christians of the first century invincible, and sustained all those in the ages which followed who were involved in the eternal, many-sided conflict between God and the devil."[1]

It was, however, useless—perhaps even dangerous—to speak too clearly. The hour of triumph would come for the disciples of the Lamb, but it would be a long time coming. Until the advent of the new Jerusalem where " there shall be no night, and they shall need no candle, neither light of sun, for the Lord God giveth them light; and they shall reign for ever and ever,"[2] there were to be countless persecutions and sufferings. It was not the duty of the seer of Patmos to define exactly the duration of these trials which, after all, were transitory. His prediction of the fall of Babylon and of the victory of the Lord sufficed.

Since it was written primarily to answer contemporary difficulties, it is natural that the Apocalypse enables us to form an idea of the state of the Churches when it was written. The letters to the Seven Churches in Asia, which provide a kind of introduction, supply most valuable information as to Christian life, heresies, and the apostolate at the end of the first century. The book itself is full of allusions which can be elucidated. It has been suggested, not without reason, that the splendid liturgy of heaven is an elaborated reproduction of the liturgy on earth; that the hymns sung by the twenty-four elders and by all the angels were those the faithful loved to sing at their meetings. If, as everything indicates, the symbol of Babylon the Great signifies Rome, the shouts of joy which welcome its fall attests the hatred which, at least in certain circles, fervent Christians bore to the idolatrous and persecuting

---

[1] L. Pirot.
[2] Apoc. xxii, 5.

empire. Examples could be multiplied. The Apocalypse is a prophecy of the end of the world; it is at the same time a document for the reign of Domitian. This ardent and passionate book shows us the spirit of the believers of that time, disturbed by the martyrdom of their brethren and impatient for the coming of divine justice, in a way that can hardly be found elsewhere.

THE GOSPEL

With the death of Domitian the persecution ended. The aged apostle could now leave Patmos and live normally again at Ephesus. It was at this time, according to tradition, that he wrote his Gospel. Saint Irenaeus[1] explains that it was to refute the heresy of Cerinthus and the much older one of the Nicolaitans that Saint John thought it necessary to give an account of " that which was from the beginning, which he had heard, which he had seen with his eyes, which he had looked upon and his hands had handled, of the Word of life ".[2] Against the heretics who taught that Jesus was not the Christ, and that the Son of God had not come in the flesh, the Gospel affirms these two dogmas: Jesus is the Messias; the Son of God is truly incarnate.

The differences between the Synoptics and the fourth Gospel have always been observed. But perhaps no one has defined them so forcefully and precisely as Clement of Alexandria, making use of an ancient tradition. Corporeal things were recorded in the Synoptic Gospels; John wrote the spiritual Gospel. But the meaning of this latter word must not be misunderstood. Spiritual is not the opposite of historical; it only implies that the meaning of history is explained and made definite and its full value brought to light.

[1] *Advers. Haeres.* iii. ii. i.
[2] 1 John i. 1.

Saint John had long meditated—for sixty years at least —on the life and teaching of the Saviour, before committing his memories to writing. On many occasions he must have had to relate the story of Jesus and recall his words. His memory was trustworthy; what he had said, what he had often repeated, was indeed what he had seen and heard, and this is what he wrote down at the request of his disciples. Nevertheless, his writing reflects his personal temperament, ardent spirit and virile love. Time had passed; his companions in the apostolate had returned to the Master and entered the mansions prepared for them; he knew that his own hour was approaching and that immortality on earth had been no more promised to him than to the other apostles. Before dying he prepared and published his Gospel to silence once for all those who did not confess Jesus. Inspired by the Holy Ghost, who " enabled him to remember all that the Lord had said ", he emphasized the Incarnation of the Word and the tragic destiny of Him who, being the light of men, was not comprehended by the darkness, was not received by His own.

The Gospel of Saint John is both a work of history and of theology, relating with precision the deeds and actions of Jesus during His earthly life, and enabling us to see fully the glory of the only Son full of grace and truth, but it is not confined solely to supplying an invaluable witness to the ministry of the Lord. It also throws a vivid light on the personal thought of the apostle. The Prologue is his work; and so also those profound observations which from time to time illustrate the narrative. " Jesus, knowing that his hour was come that he should depart out of this world unto the Father, having loved his own which were in the world, he loved them unto the end."[1]

Much has been written on the prologue of the fourth Gospel and will doubtless continue to be written. For some, these few verses contain the key to the whole work;

[1] John xiii. 1.

for others, they form a kind of extra, an adventitious element, which might very well have been omitted. The first interpretation is without doubt the true one. Would Saint John have treated the doctrine of the Word at length if it was not to be applied to the whole story of Jesus? The term Word disappears from the Gospel after the Prologue; it is replaced by synonyms; as the Word, Jesus is life and light; and He is precisely that because He is the Incarnate Word.

It is quite useless to ask again where Saint John discovered the term Word, *Logos*, and why he used it. The most learned critics have not succeeded in solving the problem. Note, however, that the apostle speaks of the Word, from the very beginning of his Gospel, as of a familiar reality; he did not consider it necessary to explain the meaning of the Word which puzzles us; in a few brief verses he recalls a whole theology. This must surely be because the faithful of Asia, at the end of the first century, were accustomed to this teaching, and the apostle, ever anxious to give a perfectly true record, was unaware of any innovation. Colossians and Hebrews at bottom develop the same doctrine which had already been out-lined in the Book of Wisdom. It is only the actual term "Word", used once in passing in the Apocalypse, that is a new element for us. Doubtless if we knew more about the Johannine communities our surprise would cease.

THE EPISTLES

The three Epistles of Saint John belong to the same period as his Gospel. From the theological viewpoint the first and longest of these Epistles is also the most important. It insists strongly on the Messianic character of Jesus and on His divinity: "Who is a liar but he that denieth that Jesus is the Christ?"[1] "Hereby know ye the Spirit of

[1] 1 John ii. 22.

God; every spirit that confesseth that Jesus Christ is come in the flesh is of God."[1] " And we have seen and do testify that the Father sent the Son to be the Saviour of the world. Whosoever shall confess that Jesus is the Son of God, God dwelleth in him and he in God."[2] " Whosoever believeth that Jesus is the Christ is born of God."[3] " This is the victory that overcometh the world, even our faith. Who is he that overcometh the world but he that believeth that Jesus is the Son of God."[4] " He that believeth the Son of God hath the witness in himself."[5] " And we know that the Son of God is come and hath given us an understanding, that we know him that is true, and we are in him that is true, even in his Son Jesus Christ. This is the true God, and eternal life."[6]

This insistence is significant. Underlying these affirmations of Saint John the negations of heretical opinion can be discerned without difficulty. His scrupulousness in recalling the true doctrine enables us to discover the errors which were advocated against it and even their widespread popularity. This first letter may have been used as a preface or commendation to the Gospel; in any case the two works supplement each other admirably. The Gospel provides the historical proof for the teaching contained in the Epistle. As befits a history, the Gospel is calm, tranquil and measured; in the foreground is the Lord who speaks and acts, while the author is simply His true and faithful witness. The Epistle, on the contrary, is a battle-cry; all are called, both old and young; all must fight against the world and those who represent it. No one can remain indifferent to the great peril with which heresy is threatening the faith.

In spite of their brevity the second and third Epistles usefully complete the teaching of the first. They not only emphasize the gravity of the errors they denounce but also

---

[1] 1 John iv. 2-3.
[2] 1 John iv. 14-15.
[3] 1 John v. 1.
[4] 1 John v. 4.
[5] 1 John v. 10.
[6] 1 John v. 20.

reveal the methods of those who promote them. We find that the authority of the apostle himself was contested in certain Churches, that certain suspect individuals refused to receive him, that being unable to communicate directly with the whole community he was forced to write to an isolated member who remained faithful. All this indicates a very disturbed situation. It is sad to think that the last days of the old apostle were troubled and perhaps disorganized by heretics, unfaithful to their Christian vocation.

II. THE LETTER OF SAINT CLEMENT

About the time when Saint John sent the Apocalypse to the Seven Churches of Asia, " the Church of God which sojourns in Rome" sent to "the Church of God which sojourns in Corinth, to those who are called and sanctified by the will of God through Our Lord Jesus Christ", a long letter, the oldest Christian document, which can be definitively dated, outside the writings of the New Testament.

This letter is anonymous; it claims to be the expression of the ideas and feelings of the whole Church of Rome. But it is clear that the Roman clergy and faithful are here represented by a mandatory; and it is equally clear—so unanimous is tradition on this point—that this mandatory is none other than Clement, who, according to Saint Irenaeus, was the third successor of Saint Peter on the episcopal see of Rome.

Why did Clement write, in the name of his brethren, to the community at Corinth? We learn from the letter that the Church at Corinth was disturbed by schisms and internal dissensions recalling the unfortunate incidents against which Saint Paul had had to fight some forty years previously. A certain number of leaders, for some unknown reason, were in revolt against the heads of the Church, the presbyters; they had deposed several, who were, however, entirely blameless; the schism had led numerous Christians astray; it brought discouragement and doubt to many, and sadness upon all. Even the non-Christians had heard of it, were scandalized and used it as a pretext for blasphemy.

The relations between Rome and Corinth were frequent. When the Roman Church heard of the troubles which divided the community at Corinth into hostile parties, it did not hesitate to intervene and recommend the benefits of peace. This intervention does not seem to have been solicited in any way by Corinth; it was a spontaneous gesture from the Romans motivated primarily by charity. " Let us then cleave to the innocent and righteous, for these are God's elect. Why are there strife and passion and divisions and schisms and a war among you? Or have we not one God, and one Christ and one Spirit of grace poured out upon us? And is there not one calling in Christ? Why do we divide and tear asunder the members of Christ, and raise up strife against our own body, and reach such a pitch of madness as to forget that we are members one of another?

" Remember the words of the Lord Jesus; for he said, ' Woe unto that man; it were good for him if he had not been born, than that he should offend one of my elect; it were better for him that a millstone be hung on him, and he be cast into the sea, than he should turn aside one of my elect.' "[1]

But charity alone is not sufficient to account for Clement's action. However fraternal his letter may be, it is impossible not to observe the authoritative tone he employs. " You therefore, who laid the foundation of the sedition, submit to the presbyters, and receive the correction of repentance, bending the knees of your hearts. Learn to be submissive, putting aside the boastful and the haughty self-confidence of your tongue, for it is better for you to be found small but honourable in the flock of

[1] 1 Clement xlvi. 4, 8.

Christ, than to be pre-eminent in repute but to be cast out from his hope. . . . Receive our counsel and there shall be nothing for you to regret. . . . But if some be disobedient to the words which have been spoken by him through us, let them know that they will entangle themselves in transgression and no little danger; but we shall be innocent of this sin."[1]

Such formulae are extremely significant; they show that their author is aware of possessing a real power to command and of a superior authority. Personally he is gentle, humble and merciful; but he has the care of sacred interests which he cannot allow to be overlooked. The Church of Rome has no desire to issue orders to the Church of Corinth; she prefers to win that Church by persuasion; nevertheless, it would be unfortunate for those who refuse to follow her counsels. This letter has been rightly acclaimed as the epiphany of the Roman primacy. Before the end of the first century Rome is using the language which will never after cease to be her own.

The evidence leads us to believe that the Church of Corinth remained thankful to that of Rome for its intervention. Between 166-175 the Bishop of Corinth, Denys, wrote to Pope Soter: "We have to-day celebrated the holy day of Sunday, and we have read your letter; we shall always continue to read it as a reminder, as well as the one that Clement previously wrote to us."[2] Thus some seventy years after the reception of Clement's Epistle, it was still read at Corinth during public worship. It would be hard to imagine a finer tribute.

III. THE LETTERS OF SAINT IGNATIUS

Saint Clement was the third successor of Saint Peter to the See of Rome. Tradition makes Saint Ignatius his second successor to the See of Antioch. At the beginning

[1] 1 Clement lvii. 1-2; lviii. 2; lix. 1-2.
[2] Eusebius, H.E. 23, 11.

B

of the second century, a persecution, of which we know neither the cause nor the precise details, broke over the Church of Antioch; the bishop was condemned to the beasts and brutally torn from his community to be sent to Rome, where he was to undergo his punishment.

His journey was long and painful; we know, however, that from time to time it was alleviated by the warm welcome given to the martyr by the Christian communities. At Smyrna in particular the Bishop Polycarp gave a brotherly welcome to his colleague from Antioch; deputations from the neighbouring Churches of Ephesus, Magnesia and Tralles also came to greet him and to recommend themselves to his prayers. Farther on, at Philippi, his reception was equally warm; the Philippians even wished, when Ignatius and his companions had to leave, to accompany them some distance out of the town.

It was in the course of this journey that Ignatius wrote the seven letters which we still possess under his name. Four of them are dated from Smyrna; they are addressed to the Churches of Ephesus, Magnesia, Tralles and Rome. The three latter were written at Troas; they were destined for the Churches of Philadelphia, Smyrna and for Polycarp, the bishop of the latter city. The authenticity of these letters has for long been discussed. To-day, with the exception of certain extremists, it seems beyond dispute.

They form one of the most valuable witnesses to Christian life at the end of the first and beginning of the second century. The witness of a soul first of all. Saint Ignatius was not a stylist; his broken phrases, his incorrect and uncompleted propositions, his unashamed neologisms would bewilder the grammarian and the rhetor. But for the Christian they are a delight; the living warmth of a great heart. The letter to the Romans is incomparable. Before coming to the end of his journey, the Bishop of Antioch felt bound to introduce himself to the Romans, to explain the motive of his visit, and, perhaps, especially to beg them to do nothing that would withhold him from martyrdom.

"For I would not have you 'men-pleasers' but 'God-pleasers' even as you do indeed please him—for neither shall I ever have such an opportunity of attaining to God, nor can you, if you be but silent, have any better deed ascribed to you. For if you are silent concerning me, I am a word of God; but if you love my flesh I shall again be only a cry. Grant me nothing more than that I be poured out to God; while an altar is still ready, that forming yourselves into a chorus of love, you may sing to the Father in Christ Jesus, that God has vouchsafed that the Bishop of Syria shall be found at the setting of the sun. . . .

"Suffer me to be eaten by the beasts, through whom I can attain to God. I am God's wheat and I am ground by the teeth of wild beasts that I may be found pure bread of Christ. Rather entice the wild beasts that they may become my tomb, and leave no trace of my body that when I fall asleep I be not burdensome to any. Then shall I be truly a disciple of Jesus Christ, when the world shall not even see my body—I long for the beasts that are prepared for me; and I pray that they may be found prompt for me; I will even entice them to devour me promptly; not as has happened to some whom they have not touched from fear; even if they be unwilling of themselves, I will force them to it. Grant me this favour. I know what is expedient for me; now I am beginning to be a disciple. May nothing of things seen or unseen envy me my attaining to Jesus Christ. Let there come on me fire, and the cross, and struggles with wild beasts, laceration, and tearing asunder, dislocation of bones, mangling of limbs, crushing of my whole body, tortures of the devil, may I but attain to Jesus Christ."[1]

The letters of Saint Ignatius are not only the witness of a profoundly Christian soul. They also provide information of an inestimable value with regard to the organization

[1] Rom. ii. 1-2; iv. 1-2; v. 2-3.

of the Christian Churches, the liturgy, the heresies, about A.D. 100. Bishop of the great city of Antioch which had recently been the primary centre of the expansion of Christianity, Ignatius had come into contact with the Churches of Asia Minor during the course of his journey. He had stayed a while at Philippi. His ardent mysticism did not hinder him from preserving a just appreciation of men and things; we might have expected it to make him an individualist concentrating on the rights of conscience. On the contrary it served to increase his respect for authority and for the role of the bishop who governs his Church together with his presbyterium and his deacons; it made him the herald of orthodoxy, anxious to avoid profane novelties and to keep intact the deposit of faith. The vigour of his testimony to the existence of the monarchical episcopate in all the Churches he visited has long been a stumbling-block for those critics who take it to be a decisive argument against the authenticity of the seven letters. Henceforth the evidence must be admitted; the letters are authentic and we shall appeal to them frequently.

IV. THE LETTER OF SAINT POLYCARP

We have seen that when Saint Ignatius was passing through Smyrna he was welcomed by its bishop, Polycarp. He remembered him so vividly that he wrote him a personal letter. It seems that shortly after the martyrdom of the Bishop of Antioch the Christians of Philippi sent to Polycarp for a complete collection of the martyr's letters. We no longer possess their request, but we still have Polycarp's answer; he sent them the letters they had asked for, and enclosed some general advice on the practice of the Christian life.

From the testimony of Saint Irenaeus we know that Polycarp was the immediate disciple of the apostles, and in

particular of Saint John. The apostles themselves had made
him Bishop of Smyrna in spite of his youth. Until the
end of his life, A.D. 155 or 156, he directed that important
Church, and among his disciples we must mention at least
the names of Florinus, who was to end his life in heresy,
and Saint Irenaeus, who on various occasions recalled his
memory. Of the numerous letters he wrote to the neighbouring Churches of Smyrna in order to strengthen them,
and to certain brethren in order to warn or stimulate
them,[1] we now only know the Epistle to the Philippians.

On the other hand, we possess the long letter, of inestimable value, addressed by the Church of God which
sojourns at Philomelium, and to all the sojournings of the
holy and catholic Church in every place. This letter is
actually the eyewitness account of Polycarp's martyrdom,
written a year after the event. This event cannot retain
us here. But the first years of his episcopate concern us,
and the Epistle to the Philippians will provide certain information with regard to the organization of the Christian
communities of Asia about the year 100.

V. THE DIDACHE OR TEACHING OF THE
TWELVE APOSTLES

The writings we have noticed up to now have the work
of definite personalities, and it has been possible to indicate
their date and place of origin with sufficient precision.

But everything becomes mysterious when we approach
the little book known under the title of *The Teaching of
the Twelve Apostles*, or better, *The Teaching of the Lord*
(taught) to the nations by the Twelve Apostles.

This book was frequently quoted in Christian antiquity.
Eusebius,[2] in his classification of the books of the New
Testament, places it after the authentic writings, among

---

[1] Eusebius, H.E. v. 20, 8.
[2] H.E. iii. 25.

the *antilegomena* together with the Epistle of Barnabas. Saint Athanasius mentions it among the books which, without being inspired, nevertheless deserved to be read in the Churches. In fact, before the fourth century Clement of Alexandria and Origen quote fragments of it as though they came from the Scriptures, and many traces of it are to be found in the early authors. In the Middle Ages and the modern period, on the other hand, it was unknown. The first printed edition appeared in 1883.

The book is divided into three parts: a moral catechesis (I-VI); a liturgical instruction (VII-X); a section on discipline (XI-XV); followed by a chapter on the last ends (XVI) by way of conclusion.

About the first part there is not much to be said. In it the author describes successively the way of life together with the duties it imposes, and the way of death, with the crimes or faults of which it is full. It is curious at the same time, that, apart from the passage I. 3–II. 1, which might be considered as an interpolation, nothing in this catechesis is specifically Christian. These pages might just as well have been written by a Jew; and there are strong reasons for thinking that originally they formed a separate work, and later were attached in a very artificial way to the succeeding chapters of the Didache.

The liturgical and disciplinary instructions are much more extraordinary. We are first told about that which concerns baptism, fast days, prayer and the Eucharist; then what must be the behaviour with regard to wandering preachers, apostles, prophets and teachers, and how the regular life of the Christian community is organized by its bishops and deacons. The formulae reproduced in the Didache on the subject of the Eucharist strike us at once by their archaic character. They make no allusion to the Body and Blood of the Lord, nor to the Last Supper. They recall certain Jewish prayers very closely; and it is all the more probable that they refer to a meal from the fact that one of them is preceded by the words: "After you are satisfied with food, thus give thanks ".[1] Not less remarkable are the counsels given on the subject of the various categories of missionaries. The author is addressing an already organized community, since it has bishops and deacons, and yet he presupposes that this community is still frequently visited by wandering preachers, and that amongst these, the prophets filled with the Holy Ghost and endowed with extraordinary gifts, deserve a special consideration.

Now we are not aware of any Christian Church, at any period, which corresponds to the conditions presupposed by the Didache. The Pastoral Epistles, which are the last writings of Saint Paul, are directed towards giving the communities stable organization. The apostle, who already in the first Epistle to the Corinthians pointed out the precautions to be taken with regard to those endowed with the gift of tongues and other charisms, in the Pastoral Epistles only mentions bishops and deacons, and recommends his disciples above all to guard the deposit. Then in the letters of Saint Ignatius, discussed in the previous section, we find every Church having as its head a bishop who is assisted by a college of presbyters and by deacons. Is there room, in the intermediary period, between the Pastorals and the Ignatian letters, for Churches which, although possessing resident heads, frequently received visits from preachers coming from goodness knows where? This is the problem of the Didache. Obviously we know too little about this period 65–100 to have the right to answer in the negative. Nevertheless it is impossible not to feel a little uncertain, and it is easily understandable that certain scholars have held the Didache to be a comparatively recent work whose author set himself out to describe an ideal of the life of the early Christian communities such as he would have liked it to have been.

On the whole, however, this hypothesis runs against many difficulties and seems impossible to sustain. "We

[1] Didache x. 1.

are led to conclude that the evolution of the Christian Churches did not take place everywhere with an absolute regularity. Some of the provinces were remote and for a long while inaccessible to progress. Where the monarchical episcopate developed soonest—in Asia Minor and Rome— the importance of the prophets and teachers could not remain intact for so long as it did elsewhere. To judge by Lucian's satire in his Life of Peregrinus (about 165) these missionaries lasted on until at least the middle of the second century; and it was precisely in his time that some charlatans ingratiated themselves among them in order to exploit the candour of the faithful. But that does not mean that similar abuses had not occurred before; and what is still predominant in the Didache is the respect rather than mistrust due towards these persons, a respect that must not lapse when those who are unknown arrive. If then we would take into account all these different aspects we shall be brought to the conclusion that the Didache cannot be earlier than the last years of the first century nor much later than the first years of the second century."[1]

VI. THE EPISTLE OF BARNABAS

The author of the Didache recalled to his readers the existence of the two ways, that of life and of death, as a means of making clear his moral teaching to them. The same procedure is employed by the unknown writer of the Epistle of Barnabas, who contrasts the way of light with the way of darkness, sometimes in terms identical with those of the Didache.

Did its author know the Didache? Or did they both draw their teaching from the same source? Or is it possible the Didache borrowed in some measure from Barnabas? All three hypotheses have had their partisans, and although

[1] A. Puech.

the second seems the most probable, the problem has not yet received a definite solution.

It is, however, only one of the many puzzles involved in the Epistle of Barnabas. This little book is addressed to a Church or group of Churches which its author knew well and in which he was carrying on a ministry. It is intended to complete the instruction of the faithful on certain important points, and although its anonymous author introduces himself on several occasions as simply one of the brethren, he is conscious of the fact that he is a teacher and has a lofty ideal of the task he has assumed. " I have therefore reckoned that, if I make it my care in your behalf to communicate somewhat of that which I received, it shall bring me the reward of having ministered to your spiritual life, and I hasten to send you a short letter in order that your knowledge may be perfected along with your faith."[1]

The teaching of the letter bears on the value of the Mosaic law. The problem had been raised from the earliest days of the Church and it had received the most varying solutions according to the diversity of the environment. In the communities of pagan origin, as a rule, the norms laid down by Saint Paul had been followed, and the Christian was declared to be definitely freed from the law. But the law itself remained; it was regarded as the word of God; the Old Testament remained for the Christians what it had been for the Jews: the inspired book. It was therefore a question of interpreting it. The Epistle to the Hebrews had clearly marked out the way for Christian exegesis. Allegory enabled the Old Testament to be conserved in its entirety and to be adapted to the exigencies of the Church.

The letter of Barnabas adopts allegorism. But with much more boldness than the Epistle to the Hebrews. It states that this has always been the true method of explaining the Law. It is not only Christians who have hence-

[1] Barn. i. 5.

forth to regard the laws of Moses as symbols; the Jews ought to have done so in the past, and for not having done so they lost their alliance with God. Did not the prophets say that God had no need of holocausts and sacrifices, that God hated the Sabbaths, the new moons and the feasts? The Jews did not understand and the Lord rejected them. " Be not like unto some, heaping up your sins and saying that the Alliance is both theirs and ours. It is ours; but they finally lost it when Moses had just received it."[1] " But let us see whether the Alliance which he sware to the fathers to give to the people—whether he really gave it. He did give it. But they (the Jews) were not worthy to receive it because of their sins. . . . It is we who have received it. Moses received it as a servant, but the Lord in person gave it to us, as the people of the inheritance, by suffering for our sakes."[2]

The condemnation of Judaism is thus irremediable. Saint Paul allowed the Law the authority of a pedagogue, charged with watching over the heir during the days of his minority; but the author of this letter affirms that from the beginning, the spiritual law was violated. Christians alone can claim the inheritance. The Jews were deprived of it from the time of Moses.

It has been truly remarked that the author is not content with coldly establishing a theory; there is a fervour in his demonstration which would be scarcely explicable unless he was intending to warn his readers against an urgent danger. At the time of writing the Jews must have shown themselves more arrogant than ever, and those of the Christians who, in spite of everything, remained attached to the Mosaic observances, were no doubt taking up the offensive once more. Hence the pathetic insistence: " We ought then to inquire into the present circumstances, and to seek out those which are able to save us (from this peril). Let us then utterly flee from all the works of

[1] Barn. iv. 6-7
[2] Barn. xiv. 1-4.

wickedness, lest they overcome us; let us hate the error of this present time, that we may be loved in that which is to come. Let us give no freedom to our souls to have leave to walk with sinners and wicked men, lest we be made like to them."[1]

At what date were the Jews able to be aggressive in this way? An indication is given on this point which would be precious if it was clearer. In the sixth chapter of his letter the writer is led to speak of the temple in which the Jews put all their hope. Did they not therefore know that God does not allow Himself to be enclosed within a sanctuary? Now Isaiah said, "Lo, they who destroyed this temple, shall themselves rebuild it. That is happening now. For because the Jews waged war, their enemies destroyed the temple; now even the servants of their enemies will build it up again."[2] The temple was destroyed in the year 70. When and how was its reconstruction decided upon? It is possible that the event should be placed at the beginning of Hadrian's reign, for according to several ancient testimonies he began by showing much good will towards the Jews. But these testimonies, however, are in general too vague to provide full certainty. Also, many critics think that the letter refers rather to the construction of the Roman colony of Aelia Capitolina, after the cruel suppression of Bar-Cochebas and his partisans, and to the building, on the very ruins of the temple, of the sanctuary of the Capitoline Jupiter. In this case, what atrocious irony the writer would be employing; speaking of that temple which in the days of its splendour was already similar to the pagan temples, and which was now replaced by a veritable temple of idols!

We may add that elsewhere, in chapter iv, there are indications which, if they were taken in their obvious meaning, would suggest that the work was composed in the reign of Vespasian or of Nerva. Out of this confusion

[1] Barn. iv. 1-2.
[2] Barn. xvi. 2-3.

there results an uncertainty from which it seems difficult to get free.

The same uncertainty exists with regard both to the personality of the writer and to his land of origin. The author nowhere names himself, and Clement of Alexandria is the first to identify him with Barnabas whose activity is well known to us through the Acts of the Apostles. No one to-day accepts this identification. The letter is thought to be of Egyptian origin, although the only reason for suggesting Egypt is because allegorical exegesis, which pseudo-Barnabas makes so much of, developed first in that country. It is thus quite possible that the letter comes from elsewhere.

But however obscure the origin of the Epistle of Barnabas may be, the work itself is none the less of great value. Even if, as is probable, it was not written before 130, and although it may only envisage a particular situation, it nevertheless throws much light on the nature of the relations which, already before the end of the first century, existed between Jews and Christians. And we shall utilize its testimony to the full extent of our needs.

VII. THE APOCRYPHAL GOSPELS

The Canonical Gospels were not the only documents written in order to recall the memory of the life and teaching of the Saviour. The prologue of Saint Luke enables us to see that, at a very early date, "many have taken in hand to set forth in order a declaration of those things which are most surely believed among us."[1] This task was carried on for a long period in the most diverse situations and with varied intentions. Hence we find by the side of the four Gospels which, at a very early date, the Church had put apart and held as inspired by the Holy Ghost, numerous apocryphal accounts which were written at

[1] Luke i. 1.

intervals between the second half of the first century and the end of the second century. It should be added that these accounts were always being revised, completed and arranged in later times. Their history therefore is most complex and obscure.

We need only mention here the most ancient of these apocryphal Gospels, those which may have been written before the end of the first century and thus provide a witness to Christian thought between A.D. 80-100.

THE GOSPEL ACCORDING TO THE HEBREWS

According to Saint Jerome,[1] a passage from the *Gospel according to the Hebrews* had already been quoted by Saint Ignatius of Antioch. This good bishop would thus be our earliest witness to this Gospel, which is also mentioned by Clement of Alexandria, Origen, Eusebius quoting Hegesippus and several other fathers. Unfortunately those who speak of it, do not say much about it, not even Saint Jerome, who affirms several times that he had translated this precious text, a copy of which he had found in the library of Caesarea, from Hebrew into Greek and Latin. One can hardly question so clear and precise a statement from the great doctor. But it remains astonishing, and it is difficult to understand how a scholar of his stature failed to find an opportunity of describing in detail what were the literary and doctrinal characteristics of the *Gospel according to the Hebrews*.

The fragments which have come down to us at least enable us to see that this Gospel was definitely orientated in a Judaeo-Christian direction. Those who first used it must have been convinced Christians, careful to put the Messiah above the prophets, but also to harmonize the two Testaments. Fr. Lagrange suggests that it was constructed from the Aramean text of Saint Matthew, which was its unique source, and that it goes back to the last years of the first century.

[1] De vir. illustr. 16.

The passages which refer to the baptism of Jesus are particularly curious. First, before the baptism: "Behold the mother of the Saviour and his brethren said to him: John the Baptist is baptizing for the remission of sins; let us therefore go and be baptized by him. But he said to them: In what have I sinned that I should go there and be baptized by him? Unless indeed that what I have just said is ignorance." Then at the moment of baptism: "It happened that when the Lord came up out of the water, the full power of the Holy Ghost descended upon him, and it said to him: My son, I awaited you in all the prophets, so that you should come and I should rest in you. For it is you who are my rest, my first-born son, who doest reign eternally."

The Gospel according to the Hebrews must not be confused with the Gospel of the Ebionites of which Saint Epiphanius speaks. This latter work, in which several of the doctrines contained in the Clementine apocrypha reappear, can scarcely be earlier than the year 200.

THE GOSPEL ACCORDING TO THE EGYPTIANS

This Gospel seems to be of a slightly more recent date than the Gospel according to the Hebrews. Clement of Alexandria knew it well, and it is also quoted by Origen, Saint Hippolytus and Saint Epiphanius. The first witness to it seems to have been the homilist who, towards the middle of the second century, wrote the work known as the Second Epistle of Clement. For in it is contained the following account which we know is to be found in the Gospel according to the Egyptians: "When the Lord himself was asked by someone when the kingdom would come, he said: When the two shall be one, and the outside as the inside, and the male with the female neither male nor female."[1]

The passages related by Clement of Alexandria confirm

[1] 2 Clem. xii. 2.

the impression produced by this quotation. We are dealing with a preacher of continence, an ascetic who condemns marriage and disapproves of all the works of the flesh. It is very doubtful if this ascetic was orthodox. However early he may have written, he is already orientated towards Gnosticism, and it is easy to understand that later heretics were fond of appealing to him. According to Saint Epiphanius, the Gospel of the Egyptians provided the Sabellians with arguments against the Trinity. Saint Hippolytus asserts that the Naassenes took their theories on the soul from it. Julius Cassien quotes the dialogue between the Saviour and Salome, etc. In these circumstances, it is difficult to believe, with Harnack, that such a work was ever officially received by the Egyptians. If it was written in Egypt, and if it succeeded in establishing itself in certain circles, it was the Gnostics and not the orthodox who ensured its fortune.

THE GOSPEL OF PETER

We may notice the *Gospel of Peter*, an important fragment of which was discovered in 1886 and published in 1892.

This fragment is composed of sixty verses. It relates the end of the trial of Jesus, His passion and resurrection, and is abruptly terminated when an account of an apparition seems about to be introduced. The story of the resurrection may be quoted as an example. " Now in the night preceding Sunday, whilst the soldiers were keeping guard, two by two, in their turn, they saw the heavens open and two men resplendent with light, come down from them and draw near the sepulchre. And that stone that had been placed before the door, rolled itself away and withdrew to one side. And the sepulchre opened and the two young men entered it. At this sight the soldiers woke up the centurion and the elders, for they also were there, keeping guard. But as they were relating what they had seen, they saw three men come out of the sepulchre, the two young men supporting the other, and a cross followed them. And the head of the first two reached the heavens, but that of him whom they led went beyond the heavens. And they heard a voice which came from heaven. It said: Have you preached to those who sleep? And from the cross was heard the answer: Yes. Then they planned together to warn Pilate of these events."

It is probable that this apocrypha was used by Saint Justin and that therefore the date of its composition cannot be later than 130–140: it may even be earlier. Its author seems to have written in Syria and to have been much preoccupied with anti-Jewish apologetics. He doubtless belonged to the orthodox Church and he wanted to bring out strongly the divinity of the Lord, even though that meant running the risk of slightly compromising his humanity. It may seem astonishing to find a Catholic Christian thus re-editing the story of the Saviour in his own way, by using and at need correcting the Canonical Gospels. But it must be recalled that before the crisis raised by the teaching of Marcion, the list of the Canonical Gospels was not yet precise, and also, even later, writers were not afraid to take great liberties with history, as is evident from the *Acts of Paul*, which Tertullian tells us were written in Asia by a priest filled with devotion for the great apostle. If only from this aspect, the Gospel of Peter deserves attention. It throws light on the attitude taken, even after the end of the first century and the passing of the last of the apostles, by certain Christians who wished to defend their beliefs, and introduced their particular apologetic interests into the very story of Jesus without shame.

VIII. THE ODES OF SOLOMON

Mystery still envelops the *Odes of Solomon* which,
first quoted in the Gnostic work *Pistis Sophia*, then known
from Lactantius, afterwards disappeared for centuries only
to be re-discovered in 1909 in an old Syriac manuscript.
The most varied hypotheses have been put forward with
regard to their origin and date of composition. In turn they
have been said to be Jewish, Catholic, Docetic, Gnostic,
Montanist canticles. They have been dated at the second
half of the first century, the beginning of the year 50, the
last years of the second century. Their first editor, Rendel
Harris, writes, for example: "The collection must go back
to the last quarter of the first century, or thereabouts."
Fr. Lebreton, on the other hand, declares: "It is without
doubt . . . in the Church of Alexandria and sometime
before Clement that the canticles which have come down
to us under the name of the Odes of Solomon, were
composed."

It seems probable that the author of the Odes belonged
to the Orthodox Church. The traces of Docetism and
Gnosticism which have been discovered in him are not
sufficiently emphatic to be ascribed to anything more than
a lack of precision in language. And it is also probable
that these canticles express the feelings of the Christians
of Asia or Syria at the end of the first century. It is not
without reason that the Johannine character of the style and
thought of the Odes has been pointed out. It is not certain
that their author, any more than Saint Ignatius of Antioch,
knew the fourth Gospel. But at least he wrote in an environment which was, as it were, saturated with the spirit
of Saint John. It is in this way that they must have prayed
in the Churches founded and watched over by the apostle.

We will now quote some fragments from these canticles. "He loves me; I should not have been able to love
the Lord, if he had not loved me (first). For who can

C

understand love, unless it be he who loves? I love the
beloved and my soul loves him. Where he takes his rest,
there shall I be, and I shall not be a stranger. For there
is no hatred with the most high and most merciful Lord.
I am mingled (with him), for the lover has found him
whom he loves. Because I love him who is the Son, I shall
become a son. Yes, he who adheres to him who does not
die becomes immortal also. And he who delights in life
shall be living. Such is the spirit of the Lord, without
untruth, who teaches men to know his ways. Be wise,
understand and watch. Alleluia! "[1]

It is not difficult to hear in this the echo of the phrases
of the Song of Songs. But these phrases are vivified in
some way by the life of him who is henceforth the beloved.
Saint Paul had already magnified " the Son of God who
loved me and gave himself for me ".[2] And Saint John has
written: " It is not we who have loved God; it is he who
first loved us, and sent his Son in propitiation for our
sins ".[3] This is the thought which motivates the author
of the Odes.

It is again the Johannine spirit which animates the
following Ode: " Fill yourselves with water from the living
well of the Lord; for it is open to you. Come, all you
thirsty ones; drink and take your rest at the well of the
Lord, for it is beautiful and pure and it brings quiet to
the soul. Its waters are far sweeter than honey, and the
honeycomb of the bees is not comparable to it, because it
issues from the lips of the Lord, and from the heart of the
Lord it draws its name. It comes infinite and invisible,
and until it is brought to them they have not known it.
Happy are those who have drunk of it and have quenched
their thirst."[4]

The images of water and of honey appear in the
Psalms. And it is Saint John who repeats the great phrase

[1] Od. iii. 2-12.
[2] Gal. ii. 20.
[3] 1 John iv. 10.
[4] Od. xxx.

of the Lord: "If any man thirst let him come to me and drink,"[1] to which this Ode corresponds so well.

With the Odes of Solomon we complete our survey of the Christian writings which can claim to be as ancient as the end of the first century or the beginning of the second. Even among the works which we have mentioned, all are not dated with certainty and some of them are not previous to a period well on into the second century. These books are only the remnants of a literature which was much more considerable. Even so they are sufficient to reveal the multiple forms of Christian activity.

Both the Churches and the faithful were concerned with the history of the past. The last apostle of Jesus who was alive was solicited by his brethren to write his memoirs and to retrace in an ineffable way the image of the Master which his memory had faithfully preserved. However different his Gospel may be from the Synoptics, it was not slow in imposing itself everywhere and in being received as inspired Scripture.

This was not the lot of the Apocryphal Gospels, which set out to satisfy a restless curiosity, and, more often, to demonstrate a thesis. Neither the Gospel according to the Hebrews, nor the Gospel according to the Egyptians, nor even the Gospel of Peter, spread beyond restricted circles in which they were written. And their doctrinal tendencies—Judaic-Christianity, Gnostic Encratism, or Docetism—ended by rendering them suspect. We know from Eusebius that about the year 200 Bishop Serapion of Antioch forbade Christians to read the Gospel of Peter which at first he thought he could authorize.

However precious the great memories of the Lord may have been for the Christians, the present life, with its anxieties and uncertainties, concerned them still more. No one in the Church had any time for writing for the sake of writing, for bothering about literature, and indeed very few of the faithful were sufficiently

[1] John vii. 37.

" educated " to have been able to do so. One wrote because one was unable to do otherwise, that is, from necessity—either to communicate news of the absent, to send advice or information to a distant community, or to warn the brethren against the seductions of error. Thus letters are the most common literary form which we find in this period. There are the letters of Saint John to the Seven Churches of Asia at the beginning of the Apocalypse; the letters of Saint Ignatius of Antioch to the Trallians, the Magnesians, the Ephesians, the Romans, the Philadelphians, the Smyrnaeans, and to Polycarp, the bishop of this latter Church; the letter of Saint Polycarp himself to the Philippians; the letter of Barnabas. Many other letters also were written by both the bishops and the faithful; these have disappeared, and it is not always clear why one has been preserved and not another.

The great interest of all these letters is the intensity of the life which animates them. Each one reveals the character of its author. Clement, who speaks in the name of the Church of Rome, is calm, tranquil, disciplined; he loves order, both that which is to be found in the universe and that which makes the strength of an army. Ignatius is passionate, ardent, tumultuous; he also is attached to harmony and he is continuously recommending unity in the Church through obedience to the bishop; but he is more of a mystic than an intellectual; he moves rather than persuades. Polycarp is content to quote Holy Scripture to correspondents whom he has never seen; the account of his martyrdom shows him to us later on as a magnificent hero in the face of death; his letter to the Philippians simply reveals his moderation and humility. Finally, pseudo-Barnabas shows the pride of scholarship united with zeal; he proves a thesis at length, but this is much more to remove a threatening danger than to give a lesson in allegorical exegesis.

This diversity of character does not prevent the identity of spirit which breathes through these letters.

All those who wrote them have one and the same faith and hope. They dwell in Ephesus, Smyrna, Antioch, Rome, Egypt; they often do not know their correspondents; but these are none the less their beloved brethren. From one end of the world to the other the Christians form a single body. " There where Jesus Christ is," declares Saint Ignatius, " there is the Catholic Church."[1] We may draw attention here to the fact that this is the first use in Christian literature of the word catholic which was destined to so great a fortune. There was not a Christian at the end of the first century who was not conscious of belonging to a Church made for the entire universe and already stretching to the extremities of the world.

But even the present, however crowded with work, was not sufficient to occupy believers. They looked towards the future. With confidence, but not without curiosity, they scrutinized the mystery of the unknown to-morrow. Saint John responded to their hopes by the Apocalypse. And others besides the apostle wrote apocalypses in their turn. The most ancient of these of which fragments have been preserved, the *Apocalypse of Peter*, must have been written about the year 140, and cannot be studied here. But it is not the only one, or the most curious.

Saint John ends his revelation with an ardent cry of desire: Come, Lord Jesus. The same cry still resounds in the Didache: it was to be frequently repeated by the Christians of the end of the first century. Doubtless many of them deceived themselves as to the true character of the coming of the Lord; they were expecting a time of extraordinary abundance, like those millenniarists whose naïve hopes were collected by Papias. " The days shall come when there shall be vines having ten thousand branches, each branch with ten thousand clusters, each cluster with ten thousand grapes, and from each grape

---

[1] Smyrn. viii. 2.

there shall be able to be drawn twenty-five gallons of wine. And when one of the saints shall have taken a cluster, another shall cry: I am a better cluster, take me, and through me bless the Lord." These marvellous images fascinated the minds of the time; they did not prevent them from desiring, more than all the others, the coming of Christ, from which they expected all good things, both those of time and of eternity.

Thus the books reveal souls. Up to now we have hardly opened the first Christian writings. We know those who wrote them and those to whom they were destined. We have before us the survivors of the generation of the apostles, and, in greater numbers, their disciples, those who received faith and hope from them. We must now question these witnesses and learn from them how they lived.

CHAPTER II

CHRISTIAN LIFE AT THE END OF THE FIRST CENTURY

The letter of Pliny. Conversion. Catechesis. The Creed. Baptism.
The Eucharist. Liturgical Prayer. Christian Life.

THE LETTER OF PLINY

IT happens by a curious accident that the document to which we owe the most complete picture of Christian life at the beginning of the second century is the work of a pagan. From 111–113 Pliny the younger was governor of the Province of Bithynia. In this official capacity he had very often to concern himself with legal actions brought against the Christians. Being doubtful about his responsibilities, he sent a letter to the Emperor Trajan to ask his advice. His letter is most instructive and deserves to be re-read.

" . . . I have never been present at any legal examination of the Christians, and I do not know, therefore, what are the usual penalties passed upon them, or the limits of these penalties, or how searching an inquiry should be made. I have hesitated a great deal in considering whether any distinctions should be drawn according to the ages of the accused; whether the weak should be punished as severely as the more robust; whether if they renounce their faith they should be pardoned, or whether the man who has once been a Christian should gain nothing by recanting; whether the name itself, even though otherwise innocent of crime, should be punished, or only the crimes that gather round it.

"In the meantime, this is the plan I have adopted in the case of those Christians who have been brought before me. I ask whether they are Christians; if they say yes, then I repeat the question a second time and a third time, warning them of the penalties it entails, and if they still persist, I order them to be taken away to prison. For I do not doubt, that whatever the character of the crime may be which they confess, their pertinacity and inflexible obstinacy certainly ought to be punished. . . .

"Others, whose names were given me by an informer, first said that they were Christians and afterwards denied it, declaring that they had been but were no longer, some of them having recanted three years before, others longer ago, and more than one so long as twenty years back. They all worshipped your image and the statues of the deities, and cursed the name of Christ. But they declared that the sum of their guilt or their error only amounted to this, that on a stated day they had been accustomed to meet before daybreak and to sing a hymn among themselves to Christ, as though he were a god; and that so far from binding themselves by oath to commit any crime, their oath was to abstain from theft, robbery, adultery, and from breach of faith, and not to refuse to return trust money that had been placed in their keeping. When this ceremony was concluded, it had been their custom to depart and meet again for food; but it was of no special character and quite harmless, and they had ceased this practice after the edict in which, in accordance with your orders, I had forbidden all secret societies. I thought it the more necessary, therefore, to find out what truth there was in these statements by submitting two women, who were called deaconesses, to the torture, but I found nothing but a debased superstition carried to great lengths.

"So I postponed my examination and immediately consulted you. The matter seems to me worthy of your

consideration, especially as there are so many people involved in the danger. Many persons of all ages and of
both sexes alike are being brought into peril of their lives
by their accusers, and the process will go on. For the contagion of this superstition has spread not only through the
free cities, but into the villages and the rural districts, and
yet it seems to me that it can be checked and set right.
It is beyond doubt that the temples, which have been
almost deserted, are beginning again to be thronged with
worshippers, that the sacred rites which have for a long
time been allowed to lapse are now being renewed, and
that the food for the sacrificial victims is once more finding
a sale, whereas, up to recently, a buyer was hardly to be
found. From this it is easy to infer what vast numbers of
people might be reclaimed if only they were given an
opportunity of repentance."[1]

Above all, the letter of Pliny reveals to us what a serious
and honest pagan was able to know about Christianity in
the year 110. It was, in truth, very little. In the streets
and public places he met men, women and children who
were said to be Christians. This name awoke no precise
memory within him; it was a sort of popular nickname
which drew its origin from Christ, who was a man condemned to death by the procurator Pontius Pilate in the
reign of Tiberius.[2]

Seeking to know a little more, he learnt that the
Christians energetically refused to take part in any of the
religious ceremonies of the day. They did not adore the
gods; they did not worship the images of the emperor; they
did not offer sacrifice. In short, they behaved like atheists;
and in a world in which public religion held the foremost
place, this was to him an unheard-of position. Doubtless
the Jews acted similarly; but then one knew that the Jews
formed a nation apart, and that, in spite of the destruction

[1] Pliny, 62-113; Epp. x, xcvi.
[2] Tacitus, *Annals* xv. 44.

of their capital and their temple, they retained certain privileges, thanks to which they could remain faithful to their ancient traditions. But the Christians were not a people; they were recruited from all social classes; they accepted as members, individuals of all ages and conditions. They were only founded yesterday, and their sect could claim no past. Their religion came out of that of the Jews; but far from living in harmony with them, the Christians had no more formidable enemy.

A still further inquiry revealed to our pagan even more astonishing things. The Christians were not content with owing their name to Christ; they adored this personage as a god. More precisely, they adored him as God, for they professed the strictest monotheism and were no less ardent than the Jews in proclaiming that there is only one God. Pagans had been long accustomed to the cult of heroes, and they even had no hesitation in paying divine honours to the emperor while he was still alive. But it seemed strange to find men giving their homage in an exclusive way to an ordinary man like themselves. Renegades would consent to curse Christ; but true Christians never did so, and even torture was unable to overcome their resistance on this point.

Two meetings held by the Christians drew the attention of Pliny. One of them took place at daybreak: hymns were sung to Christ, and an oath was taken obliging them to lead a virtuous life. The other was held later, although the precise time is not mentioned in the letter to Trajan; it was quite a harmless meal in common, of no special character. Critics have suggested that in the first of these meetings we can recognize the ceremonies common to Christian initiation; and this interpretation seems very probable. We know from Saint Justin that in the middle of the second century those about to be baptized engaged themselves to live in conformity with the doctrine of the Saviour; forty years earlier they must have done the same. The second meeting must have been the Eucharistic

Synaxis. If Pliny insisted on the harmless character of the meal in which the Christians shared, was not this because infamous calumnies were already in his time being spread abroad about them? The honest governor, not heeding the rumours, had interrogated the apostates; these had confessed that no evil took place among the Christians, and Pliny willingly admitted it. But his terminology remains vague, and one might be tempted to think that it refers to the agape. But we know nothing of the agape at this period, and it is very hard to believe that it was possible to have discussed the Christian assemblies without mentioning the principal one. Those who had ceased to take part in these meetings after Pliny's decree on secret societies are evidently renegades; the others had changed nothing in the manner of life or their habits.

Pliny says nothing of a hierarchy, apart from or above the ordinary believers. Evidently it was not very visible, and there must have been no external distinction between the leaders of the Church and the mass of the faithful. Two deaconesses are alone singled out for special mention; their ministry is not defined, but the importance attached to their testimony is clear from the fact that they were put to the torture in order to extract the truth from them.

But they extracted no more from the deaconesses than they had from the ordinary believers or apostates. Not the least crime was confessed. In spite of all the rumours, Pliny was compelled to admit the innocence of the Christians. The only things with which he could seriously reproach them were their obstinacy in practising a wild superstition, their faith, their foolish persistency which made them run the risk of death. His inquiries had been serious; they all led to the same conclusion; the Christians did not commit any crime.

This honest testimony of a pagan magistrate should be remembered. It is obviously insufficient to give us an inside view of the Christian life. We shall therefore listen now to the testimony of the disciples of the Lord themselves.

CONVERSION

Most of them were converts. The time had not yet come, nor was it near at hand, when one entered the Church, as it were, by right of birth. If, at the end of the second century, Tertullian could still declare: *Fiunt, non nascuntur Christiani*, the phrase is, *a fortiori*, exact a hundred years before. Unfortunately we have little information about the reasons which drew men to Christianity. There is no doubt that we must take into account the renewal of the religious spirit which was manifest throughout the Roman Empire at the time when the apostles began to preach the Gospel. It was then that the oriental religions took a new lease of vitality; from all parts, men and women, avid for purification, sought initiation into the mysteries of the Great Mother, of Isis, of Mithra; an immense need for salvation and regeneration possessed their souls. Christianity, which also promised a knowledge of the secrets of the beyond and offered to its chosen ones the infinite horizon of everlasting happiness, benefited from the enthusiasm which the preachers of the mystery cults stirred up everywhere.

But there was something else besides. For there was an abyss between the sensual cults of the East with their vain lustrations and the supreme demands of Christian morality. Cybele and Isis found no difficulty in accommodating themselves to the homage rendered to them by the devotees of Mithra and Adonis. The external purity which they conferred on their initiates did not exact the renunciation of the flesh and its lusts. The God of the Christians, on the contrary, was a jealous God. He claimed the adoration of His believers for Himself alone; and He required, at the same time, that they should submit themselves to the strictest discipline of the moral law. In exchange He promised them true freedom from the power of sin and the supreme joys of the redemption.

Real redemption and real liberty; that was what constituted the value of the good news preached in Christianity. Is it possible to form an exact idea to-day of the enthusiasm which the announcement of salvation was able to arouse among the slaves and the poor? When Saint Paul wrote to Corinth, to Thessalonica or elsewhere: " For ye are all sons of God by faith in Christ Jesus. . . . For there is no longer Jew nor Greek, neither slave nor free, neither male nor female. Ye are all one in Christ Jesus ";[1] when, comparing the miserable state of the faithful before their conversion with the marvellous transformation effected in them through baptism, he declared: " Be not deceived; neither fornicators, nor idolators, nor effeminate, nor abusers of themselves with mankind, nor thieves, nor covetous, nor drunkards, nor revilers, nor extortioners, shall inherit the kingdom of God. And such were some of you. But you have been washed, you have been sanctified, you have been justified in the name of the Lord Jesus and in the Spirit of our God "[2]; can one really understand the joy of all those humble, disinherited people when they heard this kind of language? The apostles doubtless preached obedience, respect for constituted authorities, submission to the severest masters; but at the same time they announced the happiness of the poor and hungry; they cursed riches and its abuse; they affirmed the suppression of all social distinctions within the unity of the children of God; and that drew!

It must be added that Christianity provided the proofs of its teaching. To the Jews, it showed that the Lord had fulfilled the sayings of the ancient prophets, and the argument was decisive to those who were willing to listen. To the pagans it brought the testimony of miracles: the Holy Ghost did not cease to manifest His action in the Church:

[1] Gal. iii. 26, 28.
[2] 1 Cor. vi. 9-11.

It filled the faithful with wonderful graces; and although from the time of Saint Paul, stern precautions had had to be taken in order to discern spirits and to regulate the activity of the charismatics which was sometimes tumultuous, yet signs and wonders remained sufficiently numerous among Christians to compel attention. Finally, to all men, Christianity offered the daily sight of holiness. The name which the faithful loved to give each other was that of brethren, and the Church was indeed a true fraternity. Not only a spiritual fraternity in the common adoption of the children of God, but of services given and accepted, of widely distributed alms, of generously shared anxieties. It was difficult to remain unaffected by this moral grandeur which was apparent for all the world to see and experience. The oath which, according to Pliny, was obligatory among Christians, obliged them above all to practise justice and charity. The majority of the faithful kept this oath.

THE CATECHESIS

When the teaching of a preacher or the result of his own reflections had determined a pagan to be converted, he was not thereby immediately introduced into the Church. The time had gone when a discourse from Saint Peter, Saint Paul, or some other apostle was sufficient to win multitudes, and was consequently followed immediately by Baptism. The Church tried to test the seriousness of the candidates who presented themselves to her, and to instruct them in her doctrine. The first chapters of the Didache give us an idea of this preparatory catechesis: it was only after the catechumen had received the teaching on the two ways that he was baptized. " There are two Ways, one of Life and one of Death, and there is a great difference between the two Ways.

" The Way of Life is this: First, thou shalt love the God who made thee, secondly thy neighbour as thyself;

and whatever thou wouldst not have done to thyself, do not thou to another. . . .

"The second commandment of the doctrine is this: Thou shalt do no murder; thou shalt not commit adultery; thou shalt not commit sodomy; thou shalt not commit fornication; thou shalt not use magic; thou shalt not use philtres; thou shalt not procure abortion, nor commit infanticide; thou shalt not covert thy neighbours' goods; thou shalt not commit perjury; thou shalt not bear false witness; thou shalt not speak evil; thou shalt not bear malice. Thou shalt not be double-minded nor double-tongued, for to be double-tongued is the snare of death. Thy speech shall not be false nor vain, but completed in action. Thou shalt not be covetous nor extortionate, nor a hypocrite, nor malignant, nor proud; thou shalt make no evil plan against thy neighbour. Thou shalt hate no man; but some thou shalt reprove, and for some thou shalt pray, and some thou shalt love more than thine own life."[1]

This teaching is continued at length. The author of the Didache tries, as far as possible, to foresee all the circumstances of the moral life and to mark out the requisite conduct in each particular case. It is curious, however, that this catechesis contains no precept that is specifically Christian: it might have been drawn up by a Jew; and only certain formulae taken from the Gospel recall its origin and destination.

THE CREED

The Didache would seem to insinuate that the candidate for Baptism received moral instruction only. This cannot be admitted. From the beginning the apostles had demanded from their converts belief in a definite doctrine. To the eunuch of Queen Candace who asked: "See, here is water; what doth hinder me to be bap-

[1] Did. 1-2.

tized? " Philip answered: " If thou believest with all thy heart thou mayest." And the eunuch made his profession of faith: " I believe that Jesus Christ is the Son of God."[1]   To believe in Jesus Christ, the Son of God—that is the essence of Christianity.

At the end of the first century and at the beginning of the second, the formula is developed.   Saint Ignatius of Antioch congratulates the Smyrnaeans on " having the firm conviction that our Lord is in truth the descendant of David according to the flesh, God's Son by the will and power of God, truly born of a Virgin, baptized by John in order to fulfil all righteousness; truly pierced by nails in the flesh for our sakes under Pontius Pilate and Herod the Tetrarch (and of the fruit of the Cross are we from His divinely blessed Passion), that He might set up an ensign for all ages through His Resurrection, for His saints and believers, whether among the Jews or among the heathen, in one body of His Church."[2]   To the Trallians the holy bishop sent these recommendations: " Be deaf therefore when anyone speaks to you apart from Jesus Christ, born of the race of David, born of Mary, who was truly born, both ate and drank, was truly persecuted under Pontius Pilate, was truly crucified and died in the sight of those in heaven and on earth and in hell, who also was truly raised from the dead."[3]

It is impossible to read these texts without being struck by their resemblance to the Christological part of our Creed. Doubtless Saint Ignatius puts more emphasis upon the reality of the birth, death and resurrection of Christ than does the Creed.   This is because he had to fight against Docetism, whose subtle errors were a menace to the faithful.   But both agree in recalling the same events of the Saviour's life.   No one enters the Church without confessing their faith in Christ.

[1] Acts of the Apostles viii. 36-37.
[2] Smyrn. i. 1-2.
[3] Trall. ix.

Neither does one enter without believing in the Trinity. In the middle of the second century, it is true, the Shepherd of Hermes still lacks precision on this point. " Above all," he declares, " believe that there is one God alone, who made all things and perfected them and made all things to be out of that which was not."[1] But this brief formula is far from exhausting the content of the Christian preaching of that time. The proof is to be found in the expressions used by Saint Clement of Rome. When he writes: " As God lives and as the Lord Jesus Christ lives and the Holy Spirit, the faith and hope of the elect "[2] he truly shows that all the faithful believed and hoped in God, in Jesus Christ their Lord, in the Holy Spirit. Similarly when he asks: " Have we not one God, and one Christ, and one Spirit poured out upon us, and are we not one people, called in Christ? "[3] is he not alluding to the formula of Baptism itself?

For in accordance with the commandment of the Lord, recorded at the end of the Gospel of St. Matthew, Baptism was conferred in the name of the Father, of the Son and of the Holy Spirit. This is the use attested by the Didache; and it does not seem that the Church ever knew or employed any other formula. Certain texts, it is true, mention a Baptism administered in the name of Christ; but when this expression is used it is not with the intention of giving an account of the actual words used in the liturgical ceremony. The Didache, after recalling, as we have just noted, that Baptism was given in the name of the Father, of the Son and of the Holy Spirit, declares a little further on: " Let none eat or drink of your Eucharist, except those who have been baptized in the Lord's Name." The Didache is simply making a distinction between Christian Baptism and other baptisms.

Recent works on the origin of the Creed seem indeed

---

[1] Shepherd. Maud. i. 1.
[2] 1 Cor. lviii. 2.
[3] 1 Cor. xlvi. 6.

D

to show that, for a time, there existed two series of formulae, the one Trinitarian, the other Christological; they existed together and developed side by side, but never became confused with each other. The most ancient baptismal creeds do not include the Christological developments; those we possess are not previous to the end of the second century, but they must represent a more ancient tradition. Thus the formula given by the papyrus of Der-Balyzeh: " I believe in God the Father Almighty, and in His only Son, our Lord Jesus Christ, and in the Holy Spirit, in the resurrection of the flesh, in the Holy Catholic Church." Thus again, the formula of the Epistola Apostolorum: " I believe in the Father, the master of the universe, and in Jesus Christ, and in the Holy Spirit, in the Holy Church, and in the remission of sins."

In Rome, at the beginning of the second century, there was doubtless utilized a formula of this sort: " I believe in God, the Father Almighty, and in Jesus Christ, His Son, and in the Holy Spirit, the Holy Church, the resurrection of the flesh." Before A.D. 150 the second article was already completed and made precise; the brief formula was replaced by a more detailed profession of faith with regard to the life and death of the Lord.

It should be noted, however, that the profession of faith demanded from candidates for Baptism was never intended to express the whole of what had been taught to them or the whole of what they believed. It resumed the essential dogmas; but, as such, its fulcrum was the formula of Baptism that is found in the Gospel. It is not surprising that at an early date an effort was made to complete it, or even to juxtapose other résumés that were more expressive, or more adapted to new needs.

BAPTISM

Baptism follows on naturally from the catechesis. The most precise testimony we have about it is that of the Didache: "Concerning Baptism, baptize thus: having first taught all that precedes (i.e. the two Ways), baptize in the Name of the Father and of the Son and of the Holy Ghost in running water. But if thou hast no running water, baptize in other water, and if thou canst not in cold, then in warm. But if thou hast neither, pour water three times on the head in the Name of the Father, Son and Holy Spirit."[1]

The minister of Baptism is not specified; but this does not imply that any believer might at any time confer the rite of initiation. Just as the preliminary instruction had to be confided to approved masters, so the administration of Baptism was a reserved ministry. Saint Ignatius expressly affirms that it is not allowable to baptize or hold the agape apart from the bishop.[2]

Baptism was habitually given by immersion. This seems to have been the traditional usage, although it may be asked whether the thousands of converts on the Day of Pentecost were not baptized by aspersion. The symbolism, so magnificently developed by Saint Paul,[3] lacks its full meaning if the neophytes do not come out immaculate from the water, in which they have, as it were, been buried. But it is remarkable that the author of the Didache knows and recommends other usages. The precautions he takes, the detailed indications he multiplies, are surprising in so ancient a document. Nothing is left to the initiative of the individual; and not only is the case where running water is unobtainable dealt with, but also that where hot water has to be used, and even that where the water has simply to be poured on the head of the person being baptized.

[1] Did. vii.
[2] Smyrn. viii. 2.
[3] Rom. vii. 3 sq.; Colos. ii. 12.

THE EUCHARIST[1]

Baptism introduces the convert into the Church. The Eucharist enables him to participate in the Body and Blood of the Lord, of which it is the mystery. It is Saint Ignatius of Antioch who provides us with the most developed testimonies on this matter and who brings out fully the place taken by the Eucharist in the Christian life of his time.

"The Eucharist," he says, "is the flesh of our Saviour Jesus Christ who suffered for our sins, the flesh which the Father raised up in His goodness."[2] Such is the expression of the Christian faith; and it is asked what are the fruits of this mystery; the answer is that it is "the medicine of immortality, the antidote that we should not die, but live for ever in Jesus Christ."[3]

At this point, the ecclesiastical character of the Eucharist should be particularly noticed. Its celebration was not left to each individual's free choice. It pertained to the bishop alone; and he was assisted by the presbyterium and the deacons. Each city had only one Church; and each Church had only one Eucharist. The participation of all the faithful in the bread consecrated by the bishop is the symbol of the unity of the Body of Christ, as that is of the unity of the Church. "See that you all follow the bishop," Ignatius wrote to the Smyrnaeans, "as Jesus Christ follows the Father; (follow) the presbyterium as you would the Apostles; and reverence the deacons as the command of God. Let no one do any of the things appertaining to the Church without the bishop. Let that alone be considered a valid Eucharist which is celebrated by the bishop, or by one whom he appoints. Wherever the bishop appears let the people be present; just as wher-

[1] A detailed criticism of the theories on the origin of the Eucharist is outside the scope of this chapter. It will be sufficient to point out that they are against the truth of revealed religion and may not be held by Catholics. [Translator.]

[2] Smyrn. vii. 1.

[3] Ephes. xx. 2.

ever Jesus Christ is, there is the Catholic Church."[1]

This doctrine could not be firmer or more established. From the moment when the convert entered the Church he became part of a social body, in which each had his place, in which the hierarchy was regularly constituted and whose unity was safeguarded by the obedience of the faithful to the bishop, to the presbyterium and to the deacons. The Eucharist itself was only valid if it was consecrated under the received forms, by the bishop or his mandatory.

The Didache is much less precise, and needs explaining. This is the way it describes the Christian meeting: "On each Lord's Day of the Lord come together, break bread and give thanks (eucharist), after confessing your transgressions that your sacrifice may be pure. But let none who has a quarrel with his fellow join in your meeting until they be reconciled, that your sacrifice be not defiled. For this is that which was spoken by the Lord, ' In every place and time offer me a pure sacrifice, for I am a great king, saith the Lord, and my name is wonderful among the heathen.'[2] Therefore elect for yourselves bishops and deacons worthy of the Lord, meek men, and not lovers of money, and truthful and approved."[3]

It is generally admitted that under the name of breaking bread it is the Eucharist that is envisaged in this passage. In support of this it is pointed out that it must be celebrated on Sundays, and this is confirmed later on by Saint Justin; that its ministers are the bishops and deacons, since these are chosen with a view to that office; and finally, attention is drawn to the word sacrifice which is applied to the breaking of bread and whose meaning is made precise by a quotation from Malachi. This analysis is surely exact. But it must be confessed that it entails a little too much deduction and that we should prefer to find a clearer description of the Eucharistic liturgy.

Many authors think that precisely this description is to

[1] Smyrn. viii. 1-2.   [2] Malachi i. 11, 14.   [3] Did. xiv-xv. i.

be found in two chapters of the Didache, the text of which deserves to be re-read:

" And concerning the eucharist (the giving of thanks), hold the eucharist (give thanks) thus:

" First concerning the cup: We give thanks to Thee, our Father, for the Holy Vine of David Thy child, which Thou hast made known to us through Jesus Thy child. To Thee be glory for ever.

" And concerning the broken bread: We give Thee thanks, our Father, for the life and knowledge which Thou hast made known to us through Jesus Thy child. To Thee be glory for ever.

" As this broken bread was scattered upon the mountains, but was brought together and became one, so let Thy Church be gathered together from the ends of the earth into Thy Kingdom, for Thine is the glory and the power through Jesus Christ for ever.

" But let none eat or drink of your eucharist except those who have been baptized in the Lord's Name. For concerning this also did the Lord say: ' Give not that which is holy to the dogs.'

" But after you are satisfied with food, thus give thanks (eucharist):

" We give thanks to Thee, O Holy Father, for Thy Holy Name which Thou hast made to dwell in our hearts and for the knowledge (gnosis) and faith and immortality which Thou hast made known to us through Jesus Thy child. To Thee be glory for ever.

" Thou, Lord Almighty, hast created all things for Thy Name's sake, and hast given food and drink to men for their enjoyment, that they might give thanks to Thee. But us hast Thou blessed with spiritual food and drink and eternal light through Thy child.

" Above all do we give thanks to Thee, for Thou art mighty. To Thee be glory for ever.

" Remember, Lord, Thy Church, to deliver it from all evil and to make it perfect in Thy love. Gather it together, sanctified, from the four winds to Thy Kingdom which Thou hast prepared for it. For Thine is the power and the glory for ever.

" Let grace come and let this world pass away. Hosanna to the God of David. If any man be holy, let him come. If any man be not, let him repent. Maranatha. Amen.

" But suffer the prophets to hold eucharist as they will."[1]

The rare beauty of these prayers cannot be denied. Filled with prophetic exaltation, they sound, in spite of reminiscences of the ancient phrases used in the Jewish synagogues, a profoundly Christian note. We experience here, in its living actuality, the love with which the Almighty Creator of the universe and Jesus His child inspired the faithful at the end of the first century. We also discover the ardent attachment of believers to the Church, which they ask may be gathered together from the ends of the earth. Both the style and the ideas are, indeed, very fine.

But they are also very mysterious. We should like to know whether these prayers ever formed part of an official liturgy, as the author seems to insinuate, or whether they merely express the notions of an individual. We should like, above all, to know whether they were used for the Eucharistic celebration or whether they are not the form for the blessing of a meal. The critics have come to no agreement about it. Some relate these two chapters of the Didache to the agape alone; others defend an exclusively Eucharistic interpretation; and others, again, think that chapter ix applies to the agape, and that chapter x, which begins with the mysterious words: " After you are satisfied, give thanks thus," applies to the Eucharist. This last interpretation certainly cannot be accepted: the parallel-ism of the phrases is too complete for us to be able to interpret one of them as applying to the blessing of a meal, and the second as applying to the Eucharistic consecration.

[1] Did. ix. x.

Both chapters are assuredly concerned with one and the same ceremony. If the two prayers are not a doublet, one of them must be recited at the beginning and the other at the end of the rite.

But what is this rite? It is a problem whose solution will probably go on being discussed for a long while yet. What is most surprising is that no mention is made in these chapters of the institution of the Eucharist by the Lord: and there is no commemoration of His death.[1] The most ancient, unquestionable description of the Eucharist, that of Saint Justin, is, in contradistinction, precise. "After having washed him who has believed and joined himself to us," writes the Apologist, "we bring him to the place where those who are called brethren are assembled together. We offer prayers in common both for ourselves and for the person who has received illumination, and for all others whosoever they may be, with all our hearts, that we might obtain, together with the knowledge of the truth, the grace to practise virtue and to keep the commandments, and so merit everlasting salvation. When the prayers are ended, we give each other the kiss of peace. Then is brought to the president of the brethren bread and a cup of water and wine. He receives them and offers up praise and glory to the Father of all things, through the Name of His Son, and of the Holy Ghost; then he returns thanks (eucharist); all the people present express their assent by saying: Amen. . . . When the president has celebrated Eucharist, and all the people have assented, the ministers whom we call deacons give to each of those who are present a portion of the Eucharistic bread and wine and water; and they carry them to those who are absent."[2]

Here no hesitation is possible. This is indeed our Eucharist, our Mass which we recognize, with its principal features already fixed. It is true that we cannot show at what moment this fixation took place, and we can only

[1] Though it is emphatically referred to as a sacrifice: cf. p. 53. [Translator.]
[2] 1 Apol. lxii.

point out that a little after the middle of the second century
Saint Justin describes the Christian rites as traditional.
Does not this fact suggest precisely that the prayers of the
Didache are too remote from the type indicated by the
Apologist, to be related to the Eucharist? The strange
resemblance between these prayers and the Jewish prayers
at table, their later utilization for prayers at table by the
author of the *De Virginitate*, the modifications introduced
into them by the author of the *Seventh Book of the
Apostolic Constitutions*, in order to give them an exact
Eucharistic meaning—does not all this prove, definitively,
they only apply to a meal? One does not dare to conclude
with certitude; but it is impossible not to be orientated
towards this interpretation.

Nor should we dare to give to this meal the name of
agape. It is certain that the agape existed at the end of
the second century. The celebrated description given by
Tertullian clearly indicates its nature and ceremonial.
Several ecclesiastical ordinances of the third and fourth
centuries, the most important of which are the Apostolic
Tradition of Hippolytus and the Canons of Hippolytus,
testify to its wide diffusion and its organization in the
Churches of the East and West. But at the end of the first
century or at the beginning of the second, there is no
evidence to prove the existence of this love feast.

From the very beginning the Eucharist was celebrated
apart from a real meal; and the reproaches addressed by
Saint Paul to the Corinthians who had tried to join such a
meal to the Lord's Supper prove this explicitly. Neither
chapter xiv of the Didache, nor the letters of Saint
Ignatius, authorize us to think that about the year 100
the rules laid down by the apostle on this point had been
contravened.

If contemporary documents do not enable us to know
the ritual used by the disciples of the apostles in celebrating the Eucharist, can we not obtain valuable information concerning it from the study of the later

liturgies? Many have thought so, and have tried to write the prehistory of the Eucharist from the liturgies of the third and fourth centuries. We cannot here enter upon an examination of the theories that have been recently propounded on this subject. We will only recall the importance that has been attributed to the anaphora quoted in the Apostolic Tradition of Saint Hippolytus. If very few critics have agreed to subscribe to the thesis of Dom Cagin, who saw in this text the anaphora used by the apostles themselves, or at least by their first disciples, when celebrating the Eucharist, all are agreed in considering it as one of the most precious witnesses to the ancient Roman liturgy. According to Lietzmann, the anaphora of Hippolytus is only equalled in importance by the anaphora of Serapion. These two venerable witnesses, he suggests,[1] are a proof of the existence of two primitive forms of the Eucharist: the Roman form, represented by Hippolytus, is derived from Saint Paul and from the worship carried out in the Churches organized by him, or under his influence; the Egyptian form, conserved in the anaphora of Serapion, goes back to the Didache and even to the first community at Jerusalem. If the prayers of the Didache make no allusion to the death of Jesus, that is precisely because the Eucharist, celebrated according to this rite, does not reproduce the Last Supper, but recalls the ordinary meals taken by Jesus and His disciples during His mortal life. Saint Paul, on the other hand, is the inventor of the system which binds the Eucharistic celebration to the memory of the Supper. Since Saint Paul's theology finally spread everywhere, the tradition of Jerusalem, which was at first kept up in Egypt, was unable to endure in its primitive purity. All the liturgies known to-day have undergone the influence of that of Hippolytus.

This hypothesis is certainly interesting. But its

[1] His suggestion cannot, of course, be accepted by a Catholic. [Translator.]

foundations are so much the more fragile owing to the fact that we do not know the exact meaning of the prayers of the Didache. Historians are right in seeking the traces of ancient institutions in documents that are relatively recent. But is it not a kind of paradox to claim that the Eucharist was ever independent of the memory of the Supper and of that of the Saviour's death?

Other critics have preferred to seek the antecedents of the Eucharist in the pagan mystery cults, and they try to explain the Christian liturgy as a result of more or less conscious imitation of sacred meals which figured in those mystery religions. But the analogies upon which they based their theories proved singularly deceptive.

" It has not been proved that the saviour-gods of syncretism were literally dead and risen gods, that the mysteries intended to commemorate their passion efficaciously, that the initiates attributed to this passion and its commemoration a sacramental efficaciousness, that this efficaciousness derived from the union between the faithful and the passion of the gods, that this union was realized by means of a sacrificial meal whose essential rite consisted in the distribution of hallowed bread and a cup of consecrated wine, and finally that the salvation thus obtained was of a spiritual and individual order, assured for all eternity."[1] In short the Eucharist is a specifically Christian ceremony. Instituted by Christ, it has never ceased to be regarded by the Church as the memorial of His death and the sacrament of His Body and Blood.

LITURGICAL PRAYER

In the absence of the prayers for the celebration of the Eucharist, we know at least and we must quote, as characteristic of Christian piety at the end of the first century, the great prayer that Clement inserted in his letter to the

[1] L. Coppens.

Corinthians. By its form and style it is a true liturgical prayer. Like the whole letter it is not the expression of the individual ideas of Clement, but it expresses the thought of the Roman Church, and it does so with the solemn and calm majesty which was to remain for the future the mark of the liturgy of Rome.

" May the Creator of the Universe guard unhurt the number of His elect that has been numbered in all the world through this beloved child Jesus Christ, through whom He called us from darkness to light, from ignorance to the full knowledge of the glory of His Name. (Grant us) to hope in Thy Name, the source of all creation.

" Open the eyes of our heart to know Thee, that Thou alone art the Highest in the highest (heavens), the holy who doth rest among the saints. Thou dost humble the pride of the haughty; Thou dost destroy the calculations of nations; Thou dost raise up the humble and abase the lofty; Thou makest rich and makest poor; Thou dost slay and make alive. Thou alone art benefactor of spirits and art God of all flesh. Thou dost see to the depths of the abysses; Thou dost scrutinize the work of men. Helper of those in danger; Saviour of the desperate; Creator and watcher over every spirit. Thou dost multiply nations upon earth and hast chosen out from them all those that love Thee through Jesus Christ Thy beloved child, and through Him hast Thou taught us, made us holy, and brought us to honour.

" We beseech Thee, Master, to be our help and succour. Save those of us who are in affliction, have mercy on the lowly, raise up those that are fallen, show Thyself to those in need, heal the sick, turn again the wanderers of Thy people, feed the hungry, ransom our prisoners, re-establish the weak, comfort the fainthearted. Let all the nations know Thee, that Thou art God alone, and that Jesus Christ is Thy child, and that we are Thy people and the sheep of Thy pasture.

" For Thou through Thy operations make manifest

the eternal order of the world. Thou, Lord, didst create the earth. Thou that art faithful in all generations, righteous in judgment, wonderful in strength and majesty, wise in Thy creation, and prudent in establishing Thy works, good in the things which are seen, and gracious among those that trust in Thee, O merciful and compassionate, forgive us our iniquities and unrighteousness, and transgressions and shortcomings. Reckon not every sin of Thy servants and handmaids, to do the things which are pleasing and good before Thee and before our rulers.

"Yea, Master, make Thy face to shine upon us in peace for our good, that we may be sheltered by Thy mighty hand, and delivered from all sin by Thy uplifted arm, and deliver us from them that hate us wrongfully. Give concord and peace to us and to all that dwell on the earth, as Thou didst give to our fathers who called on Thee in holiness with faith and truth, and grant that we may be obedient to Thy almighty and glorious Name, and to our rulers and governors upon the earth.

"It is Thou, Master, who has given the power of sovereignty to them, through Thy excellent and inexpressible might, that, knowing the glory and honour given to them by Thee, we may be subject to them and in no way resist Thy will. Grant to them, Lord, health, peace, concord, firmness, that they may administer the government which Thou hast given them without obstacle. For it is Thou, Master, heavenly King of eternity, who hast given to the sons of men glory and honour and power over the things of the earth. Do Thou, O Lord, direct their counsels according to that which is good and pleasing before Thee, that they may administer with piety in peace and gentleness the power given to them by Thee, and may find mercy in Thine eyes.

"Thou alone hast the power to do these things and to give us even few better things. We praise Thee through Jesus Christ, the high priest and guardian of our souls, through whom be glory and majesty to Thee, both now and for all generations and for ever and ever. Amen."[1]

It has been justly remarked " that this prayer, written in the most evil days of Domitian's reign, and yet full of such peace, submission, humility and trust, cannot be read without emotion. Princes are reverenced and intermission is made for them; they are envisaged only as the depositaries of that sovereign power which is venerated. And above and beyond all the miseries of this world, the mind is fixed upon the most high and most holy God from whom all good things proceed. The Christian adores this immense grandeur; he contemplates it in the creation and government of the world, in the merciful solicitude with which God has guided ' our forefathers,' and above all in that wonderful calling which has the elect to pass from darkness to light, from ignorance to the glory of the divine Name, through the beloved Son, Jesus Christ."[2]

In order to estimate the distance which separated Christian piety from that which invoked idols, it would be necessary to compare the great prayer of Clement with pagan examples. We certainly possess pagan prayers characterized by a profoundly religious sense. But is there a single one that is at the same time so calm, generous and exalted? Easily and without excitement, the Christian enters into the domain of invisible realities; he does not think himself obliged to multiply eloquent terms, paraphrases or words for effect, in order to address God. God is, without doubt, his Creator and his Lord; but He is also, and above all, his Father.

Also, each believer prays according to his temperament and way of life. The letters of Saint Ignatius do not contain his prayers; but reading them it is not difficult to imagine what they must have been like: ardent and passionate, full of love for Christ who deigned to call His disciple to martyrdom. We should scarcely need to transpose some of his expressions. His letters reveal his piety,

[1] 1 Clem. lix. 2-lxi. 3.
[2] J. Lebreton.

which is that of one of the most generous souls that the Saviour has ever called to His service.

Saint Polycarp, the disciple of Saint Ignatius, is perhaps less spontaneous. The story of his martyrdom recalls the prayer he made to the Lord before being burnt alive. It has that liturgical and solemn tenor which characterizes the prayer of Clement: " O Lord God Almighty, Father of Thy beloved and blessed child, Jesus Christ, through whom we have received full knowledge of Thee, the God of angels and powers, and of all creation, and of the whole family of the righteous who live in Thy presence, I bless Thee, that Thou hast judged me to be worthy of this day and hour, worthy to share, among the number of the martyrs, in the cup of Thy Christ, for the Resurrection to everlasting life, both of soul and body, in the immortality of the Holy Spirit. And may I, to-day, be received among them in Thy presence, as a rich and acceptable sacrifice, so that the destiny which Thou, O God of truth who doth never lie, hast prepared before-hand for me, and which Thou hast enabled me to foresee, may now be fulfilled. For this grace and for all things I praise Thee, I bless Thee, I glorify Thee, through the everlasting and heavenly high priest, Jesus Christ, Thy beloved child, through whom be glory to Thee with Him and the Holy Spirit, both now and for the ages that are to come. Amen."[1]

It is probable that this prayer was rewritten by the authors of the letter and that it is they who have given it this noble solemnity; none the less it cannot be doubted that it is an authentic expression of the soul of Saint Polycarp: at once generous and tranquil, loving and reasonable. For this is how the Bishop of Smyrna appears to us in his Epistle to the Philippians, and in the Acts of his martyrdom, and in the moments before his last agony.

Almost unconsciously, we have passed from liturgical

[1] Martyr Polyc. xiv.

to individual prayer. In the period we are studying there is as yet no clear separation between the two. He who presided over the assembly of the brethren and celebrated the Eucharist could pray as much as he wished; on the immutable theme of thanksgiving he embroidered many variations. And it will be easily understood that a bishop like Polycarp or Clement, accustomed to gathering together the prayers of his brethren, would naturally acquire the manner of the liturgical prayers. Similarly, one can understand that a simple believer would like to use the expressions he had already heard and to repeat the words he had retained from the services in the Church.

But already, together with the prayers freely composed by each person's piety, there seems to have been an official prayer that ran throughout the whole Church. When His disciples had asked Him to show them how to pray, the Saviour had answered by teaching them the Our Father. According to the Didache, the faithful had to repeat this prayer:

" Do not pray as the hypocrites, but as the Lord commanded in His Gospel, pray thus: Our Father, who art in heaven, hallowed be Thy name. Thy Kingdom come. Thy will be done, as in heaven so on earth. Give us to-day our daily bread, and forgive us our debt as we forgive our debtors, and lead us not into temptation, but deliver us from evil. For Thine is the power and the glory for ever. Pray thus three times a day."[1]

If we could really take the Didache into account, this passage would show the place held by the Lord's Prayer in the religious life of Christians towards the end of the first century. If, as well as being privately recited three times a day, it was also publicly recited in the liturgy of Baptism and the Eucharist, that place must have been even more extensive. It is certain that the Lord's Prayer came early into the liturgy, but we do not know at what date it was introduced.

[1] Did. viii.

CHRISTIAN LIFE

Prepared for Baptism by the catechesis, introduced into the Church by the sacrament of initiation, nourished by the Body and Blood of the Lord, the new Christian was henceforth transformed. Not only did his religious life receive a more precise orientation, but his entire existence acquired a purpose that had been, up to then, unknown.

His prayer was continuous. As Aristides wrote, about the year 140, the Christians " every morning and every hour sing of God and praise Him for His goodness towards them; and they likewise offer Him thanks for their food and drink. And if, from among them, a just man goes out of this world, they rejoice and give thanks to God, and they follow his body, as if it was from one place to another. And when a child is born to one of them, they praise God; and if the child dies young, they praise God with all their strength because it has gone through the world without sin. But if they see that one from amongst them has died in his iniquity and his sins, they weep bitterly over him and groan, because he has gone to receive his punishment."[1]

In the same way the whole of the Christian life was directed towards heaven. An unknown Apologist, the author of the letter to Diognetus, who is often ranked among the Apostolic Fathers, although he doubtless belongs to a more recent date, has portrayed this life in an ideal picture which may be recalled here: " They dwell in their own native countries, but as if sojourners in them; they share all things as citizens, and suffer all things as strangers. Every foreign country is their fatherland, and every fatherland is a foreign country. They marry like all men; they bear children, but they do not expose their offspring. They offer free hospitality, but guard their

[1] Apol. xv.

E

purity. Their lot is cast in the flesh, but they do not live after the flesh. They pass their time upon the earth, but they have their citizenship in heaven. They obey the appointed laws, and they surpass the law in their own lives. They love all men and are persecuted by all men. They are unknown and they are condemned. They are put to death and they gain life. They are poor and make many rich; they lack all things and have all things in abundance. They are dishonoured and are glorified in their dishonour; they are spoken evil of and immediately after their justification is proclaimed. They are abused and give blessing in return; they are insulted and give respect. Only doing good, they are punished as male-factors; when they are punished they rejoice as men who receive life. They are warred upon by the Jews as foreigners and are persecuted by the Greeks, and those who hate them cannot state the cause of their enmity.

" To put it shortly, what the soul is in the body, that the Christians are in the world. The soul is spread through all members of the body, and Christians through-out the cities of the world. The soul dwells in the body, but is not of the body, and Christians dwell in the world, but are not of the world. The soul is invisible, and is guarded in a visible body, and Christians are recognized when they are in the world, but their religion remains in-visible. The flesh hates the soul, and wages war upon it, though it has suffered no evil, because it is prevented from gratifying its pleasures, and the world hates the Christians, though it has suffered no evil, because they are opposed to its pleasures. The soul has been shut up in the body, but itself sustains the body; and Christians are confined in the world as in a prison, but themselves sustain the world. The soul dwells immortal in a mortal tabernacle, and Christians sojourn among corruptible things, waiting for the incorruptibility which is in heaven. The soul when evil treated in food and drink becomes better, and Christians when buffeted day by day increase more and more. God has appointed them to so great a post and it is not right to desert it."[1]

There is no doubt that this picture is strongly idealized. Reminiscences of Stoicism are to be found in it; and its anonymous author purposely multiplies antitheses in order to bring out the grandeur and novelty of the Christian life. But when one has made every allowance for idealization, the fact remains that the letter to Diognetus claims to describe a real mode of life; and it does so.

In the old pagan world Christianity was truly the leaven which leavened the whole, and the believers in Jesus made themselves recognized as well by the charity which united them to each other, as by their incessant effort to practise virtue. They were not all saints; but this name of saints, which they used from the beginning as their designation, expresses, at best, their tendency. They were conscious of forming a holy people. The Church to which they belonged was a holy church.

In the same way they constituted a fraternity of love and assistance. " They recognized as father one and the same God; they have quenched their thirst from the same spirit of holiness, and having come out from the same depths of ignorance, they have seen, with wonder, the shining of the same light of truth."[2] And they helped each other mutually, from one end of the world to the other. " From community to community there was a constant exchange of guests, of missionaries, of help, as well as of advice, edification and affectionate control."[3] The letters of Saint Ignatius and the letter of Saint Clement to the Corinthians reveal this same sense of profound solidarity, as a result of which no Christian could suffer without the whole body of the Church experiencing a suffering and being troubled also. It was not only a question of sending material help to the indigent and of multiplying

[1] Ep. ad Diogn. v.-vi.
[2] Tertullian. Apolog. xxxix. 9.
[3] P. Batiffol.

collections for the poor communities. It was much more a question of ensuring everywhere the benefit of peace and concord, of sharing the sorrows and joys of all, of associating together in difficulties as well as in successes. The Christian life was a life of charity.

CHAPTER III

THE CHURCH AND THE CHURCHES: THE HIERARCHY

The Churches. The Church. The Hierarchy. Apostolic Succession.
The Episcopate. The Itinerant Preachers. Christian Unity. The
Roman Church.

THE Christian is not isolated; he is a member of a Church.
This was the case from the beginning, and when it developed, Christianity only accentuated, if possible, its social
character. Like those of Saint Paul, the letters of Saint
Ignatius of Antioch and of Saint Polycarp of Smyrna are
addressed to a Church; the letter we attribute to Saint
Clement was sent by the Church of Rome to the Church
of Corinth, and the account of Saint Polycarp's martyrdom
was written by the Church of Smyrna for the Church of
Philomelium and for all the Christian communities
belonging to the Holy Catholic Church.

THE CHURCHES

Normally there was a Church for every city. Each town
had its community, to which all the faithful belonged. In
contrast with the Jewish synagogues, where believers were
grouped according to their origin and social rank, and
with the pagan " colleges ", which only assembled the
members of a single corporation, the Church was the
assembly of all those in the city who recognized Christ.
All the Christians of the town, however large it might be,

formed one and the same confraternity, which bore the name of the city itself. A cult, like that of Mithra, developed by means of chapels and confraternities, dividing up regularly when the number of the devotees of the god increased; the Christian law was that there should be only one Church in each city.

It is remarkable that, at that early date, Saint Ignatius should have taken the title of Bishop of Syria; we know that in reality he was Bishop of Antioch, and that there were other Churches in his time quite close to that of Antioch. By presenting himself as Bishop of Syria, Saint Ignatius was not trying to disregard the rights of his colleagues; he uses an emphatic expression to designate the community of which he was head; at the same time he witnesses to the interest taken by the Church of the metropolis in the faithful of the neighbouring cities.

Theoretically each Church was organized so as to be self-sufficient; it had its head, its clergy, its faithful; it possessed its resources, which it acquired from charity; it took care of its poor, its widows, its orphans; it celebrated its liturgy in which all took part. But actually its activity and solicitude were spread far beyond the limits of the city.

THE CHURCH

If there are Churches, if there is a Church in each city, there is only one Church in the world. All the faithful, to whatever local group they belong, are members of this one Church, which is the very body of Christ. Saint Paul seems to have been the first to have given a magnificent exposition of the theory of Christian unity.

"Through Christ we both have access to one Spirit unto the Father. Now therefore ye are no more strangers and foreigners, but fellow citizens with the saints and of the household of God; and are built upon the foundation of the apostles and prophets, Jesus Christ himself being the chief corner-stone; in whom all the building fitly framed together groweth unto an holy temple in the Lord; in whom ye also are builded together for an habitation of God through the Spirit."[1]

Saint John, for his part, reminds us that Christ died: "For that nation (the Jewish); and not for that nation only, but that also he should gather together in one the Children of God that were scattered abroad."[2]

And he quotes the Lord's prayer for unity: "Neither pray I for these alone, but for them also which shall believe on me through their word; that they all may be one; as thou Father art in me and I in thee, that they also may be one in us; that the world may believe that thou hast sent me."[3]

The Church never ceased to pray in this way; the author of the Didache asks that: "As this bread that is broken, once scattered on the mountains has been gathered together and has become one, so may thy Church be gathered together from the extremities of the earth into thy kingdom." "Be mindful, O Lord, of the Church, and deliver her from all evil and perfect her in thy love. Gather her from the four winds, sanctified, into thy Kingdom which thou hast prepared for her."[4]

Similarly Saint Clement of Rome prays that the Creator of the universe shall keep intact the number of the elect which he has decreed.[5]

And this prayer is heard: "There where the bishop appears, writes Saint Ignatius of Antioch, there the collectivity (of the faithful) must be, just as there where Jesus Christ is, there is the Catholic Church."[6]

We must note the term Catholic in this passage for it is the first time it appears in a Christian writer. Doubtless when Saint Ignatius uses it he is not thinking of opposing the universal Church to heretical meeting-places; with him it is a question only of opposing the local Churches to the universal Church; but the latter receives henceforth

---

[1] Ephes. ii. 16-22.   [2] John xi. 15.   [3] John xvii. 20-21.
[4] Did. ix. 5; x. v.   [5] 1 Clem. lix. 2.   [6] Smyrn. viii. 2.

the name it will never cease to bear and which will be its true claim to glory for ever.

THE HIERARCHY

In order that unity shall be maintained in the Church there must be an organization, a hierarchy. This is especially true in the local Church, and no one perhaps insisted more on this than Clement.

" Let us make our campaign, men and brethren, with all possible application, under the irreproachable command of Christ. Consider the soldiers who serve under our leaders; what discipline, what docility, what submission in executing orders. All are not eparchs, chiliarchs, hecatontarchs, pentecontarchs and so on, but each in his own rank carries out the orders of the Emperor or of the leaders. The great cannot do without the small, nor the small without the great; in every species of things there is a certain mixture in which its utility resides. Take the example of our body; the head without the feet is nothing; similarly the feet are nothing without the head. The least members of our body are necessary and useful for the whole body; or rather all compose and serve by a unanimous subordination the health of the whole body. Therefore let the body which we form in Jesus Christ be preservèd in its integrity; let each be subordinate to his neighbour, according to the charism with which he has been invested. Let the strong take care of the weak and the weak respect the strong; let the rich assist the poor and the poor thank God for having given them someone to supply their needs. Let the wise man manifest his wisdom not in words but in good actions; let the humble man not bear witness in his own favour, but leave that task to another. Let the chaste man not boast knowing that it is another who grants him continence."[1]

[1] 1 Clem. xxxvii-xxxviii.

Such are the principles. With a thoroughly Roman instinct for discipline Clement compares the Church to an army and asks that the faithful observe the same subordination to and respect for their leaders that soldiers have for their officers. The metaphors borrowed from military life were already familiar to Saint Paul; they are renewed here because the author of the letter to the Corinthians enters into details and could not refrain from proclaiming his admiration for the Roman army.

THE APOSTOLIC SUCCESSION

It would, however, have been inadequate merely to have given a general recommendation to obedience, and Clement goes on to define the leaders to whom Christians must subject themselves. "The apostles," he says, "received the Gospel for us from the Lord Jesus Christ. Jesus Christ was sent from God. The Christ therefore is from God and the apostles from the Christ. These two things, then, were in accordance with the appointed order of God's will. Having therefore received their instructions from the Lord Jesus Christ, and being fully convinced by his resurrection, and with faith confirmed by the word of God, they went forth in the assurance of the Holy Ghost, preaching the good news that the Kingdom of God is coming. They preached from district to district, and from city to city, and they appointed their first converts, testing them by the Spirit, to be bishops and deacons of the future believers. . . . Then they added this rule that after their death other approved men should succeed to their ministry. . . . Those were thus appointed by the apostles, or later on by other eminent men, with the consent of the whole Church, having ministered to the flock of Christ without blame, humbly, peaceably, and disinterestedly, and for many years have received a universally favourable testimony."[1] These were the contemporaries of Clement, and

[1] 1 Clem. xlii., xlv.

he is assured that on their death they will be replaced according to the same rule that was applied at their election.

This fundamental passage gives us the mind of Clement and of the Roman Church with regard to the apostolic succession. So long as the apostles lived it was they who governed the Churches. But at the time when Clement was writing to the Corinthians, all of them, with the exception of Saint John, were dead. Nevertheless the Church still carried on under the direction of those whom they had chosen. Election was the rule; the bishops were the electors, and the community gave its consent. In the Didache[1] the function of the community seems to have been wider, for it is invited not merely to approve the choice made by the surviving leaders but to choose bishops and deacons for itself.

THE EPISCOPATE

Bishops and deacons, these seem to have been the only representatives of the hierarchy that Clement and the author of the Didache were aware of. They had already been mentioned by Saint Paul in the beginning of the Epistle to the Philippians, and he gives many instructions concerning them in the Pastoral Epistles. Each community would thus seem to have been governed and directed by a college of bishops, or as they are called in the letter to the Corinthians, presbyters, and by deacons subordinated to the bishops.

Both these members of the hierarchy were chosen for their virtues, their gentleness, disinterestedness and sincerity. They had to be tried men; and those who elected them, even more than those who laid their hands on them, incurred from this fact a grave responsibility. The hierarchy was recruited in virtue of a supernatural designation, on a charism, but on a harmony of moral qualities which

[1] Didache xv. 1.

the members must possess. If we put aside certain excep-
tions, there is no evidence that the leaders of the Church,
though ordained or consecrated by a sacramental rite after
election, were personally designated by God. From the
beginning, Saint Paul chose his collaborators by his own
decision. He separated himself from John Mark and took
Silas with him. He added Titus, Timothy, Luke and
others. Not one of his companions was imposed on him
by extraordinary graces. It was the same after the death
of the apostles; those who governed the communities were
not endowed with miraculous gifts, and, like other men,
they could fail.

The ministry of the bishops and deacons has a twofold
aspect of teaching and worship. The Didache chiefly insists
on their liturgical functions; it is after having described
the breaking of bread on Sunday that its author adds:
"Appoint therefore for yourselves bishops and deacons
worthy of the Lord."[1] Saint Clement, comparing the
Christian with the Levitic priesthood, writes in a similar
way: "The Master has commanded us to celebrate sacrifices and services, not thoughtlessly or disorderly, but at
fixed times and hours. He has himself fixed by his supreme
will the places and persons whom he desires for these
celebrations, in order that all things may be done piously
according to his good pleasure and be acceptable to his
will. . . . For to the High Priest his proper ministrations
are allotted, and to the priests the proper place has been
appointed, and on Levites their proper services have been
imposed. The layman is bound by the ordinances for the
laity."[2]

It is Saint Ignatius who most emphasizes the function
of the bishop in the liturgy. No one has brought out his
preponderance more vividly and the obligation of the
faithful to participate in the Eucharist he offers. "See
that you all follow the bishop as Jesus Christ follows the
Father," he writes to the Smyrnaeans, "and the presbytery

[1] Didache xv. 1.   [2] 1 Clem. xl. 2, 3, 5.

as if they were the Apostles. And reverence the deacons as the law of God. Let no one do any of the things pertaining to the Church without the bishop. Only regard as valid that Eucharist which is offered by the bishop or his delegate. Wherever the bishop appears let the congregation be present; just as wherever Jesus Christ is, there is the Catholic Church. It is not lawful either to baptize or to hold an agape without the bishop; but whatever he approves, this is also pleasing to God. In this way everything you do will be secure and valid."[1]

The episcopate is also destined to teach and to be the agent of discipline. Clement who, in his letter to the Corinthians, sets himself to correct disorders and disobedience lays the emphasis on the warnings which the presbyters give. " Let us receive correction, which none should take amiss, beloved. The admonition which we make one to another is good and beyond measure helpful, for it unites us to the will of God."[2] " Submit to the presbyters, and receive the correction of repentance, bending the knees of your hearts. Learn to be submissive. . . . For it is better for you to be found small in the flock of Christ, than to be pre-eminent in repute but to be cast out from His hope."[3]

Ignatius, who has the heresies chiefly in mind, gives more emphasis to the action of the bishop in doctrinal matters. " For as many as belong to God and Jesus Christ —these are with the bishop. And as many as repent and come to the unity of the Church—these also shall be of God, to be living according to Jesus Christ."[4] It is true that his expressions sometimes lack precision. In the letter to the Philadelphians, for example, he recalls a discussion he had had with the Docetists. These claimed to rely exclusively on the authority of their archives, i.e. on the Gospels. Ignatius admitted the same principle, or at least he recognized the formative value of the Gospels. But

[1] Smyrn. viii.
[2] 1 Clem. lvi. 2.
[3] 1 Clem. lvii. 1-2.
[4] Philad. iii. 2.

his adversaries drew him into interminable controversies about the real meaning of what was written that ultimately he contented himself with affirming: "To me the archives are Jesus Christ, the inviolable archive is His Cross and Death and Resurrection and the faith of which He is the Author."[1] We should have preferred him to have appealed to the authority of the bishop, the sole authorized interpreter of Scripture. In the case of heretics who argue about texts, there is the Church represented by the bishop. Ignatius does not say so with sufficient clarity; but taking his doctrine on the episcopate as a whole there is no room for equivocation; apart from the bishop there can only be error.[2]

Clement and the Didache, we noticed, seem only to know of a hierarchy of two degrees; presbyters or bishops and the deacons. Saint Ignatius, on the contrary, constantly mentions a hierarchy of three degrees. In all his letters the bishop is quite distinct from the presbyters; he is superior to them and the true head of the Christian community. "Let all respect the deacons as Jesus Christ, even as the bishop is also a type of the Father, and the presbyters as the council of God and the College of the Apostles."[3] "The faithful must be subject to the bishop, to the precious spiritual crown of the presbyterium, to the holy deacons."[4] "The presbyterium is attuned to the bishop as the strings to a harp, and the whole Church sings harmoniously in concord as a single choir and with one voice."[5]

This hierarchy of three degrees is for Ignatius an accepted fact, a traditional reality, to which he need not revert and which does not require discussion. Everywhere, at Smyrna, Tralles, Philadelphia, Magnesia and Ephesus there is a bishop who is above the presbyteral body and

---

[1] Philad. viii. 2.
[2] Ephes. iv. 1-2; Magn. iii. 2; Trall. ii. 1-2; Smyrn. viii. 2, ix. 1, etc.
[3] Trall. iii. 1; cf. Smyrn. viii. 1; Polyc. vi. 1.
[4] Magn. xiii. 1.
[5] Ephes. iv.

there are deacons who form an inferior degree of the hierarchy. For how long has this existed? Who gave this organization to the communities? These problems did not occur to the Bishop of Antioch who took the Church as he found it, and who answered heretics, the friends of novelty and disorder, mainly by pointing out the actual benefits and fittingness of the established situation.

It has been remarked that Ignatius's letter to the Romans seems to constitute an exception in his correspondence. For in this letter alone he makes no mention of the bishop and of the submission due to him. It is addressed in an impersonal manner " to the Church . . . which has the presidency in the country of the land of the Romans ". This mode of address has been related to that which opens the letter to the Corinthians; this letter was sent, as we have seen, from the Church of God which sojourns in Rome. It has therefore been said that, at the time of Ignatius, the monarchical episcopate, already known in Antioch and Asia Minor, was not as yet organized in Rome and in other Churches such as Philippi.[1]

This conclusion does not follow; far from it. For it is remarkable that the letter addressed by the Church of Rome to the Church of Corinth became known in history by the name of Clement; as such it is quoted by Denis of Corinth about the year 160. The same name of Clement was used later on to recommend a most abundant and varied apocryphal literature. These facts cannot be explained except by admitting a unique importance to the personality of Clement. The letter to the Corinthians is assuredly the work of a single author who makes himself the interpreter of the Roman community. We have still less right to refuse that authorship to Clement, since he is known to us from the ancient Roman episcopal lists as the second successor to Saint Peter.

For from the middle of the second century the Roman Church possessed a list of its bishops, and was thus enabled

[1] Polycarp. Cf. Philip. v. 3.

to trace them back to Saint Peter. It was the same in other important Churches of the East and West. About the year 150, Hegesippus, in the course of a long journey he had undertaken in order to verify the sound tradition of the apostolic preaching, found at Jerusalem the authentic succession of its bishops from the time of James the Just. At Corinth and at Rome he did the same. We know from Saint Denis of Corinth the list of Athens which goes back to Denis the Areopagite; from Saint Irenaeus the list of Rome. Wherever it is found, the unitary episcopate stands out as the legitimate heir of a tradition; nowhere do we find the least trace of a conflict, of a transformation, of a revolution which substituted for the college of presbyters the centralizing authority of a monarchical episcopate.

Before the end of the second century everyone knew, everyone recalled that the apostles had instituted bishops in the communities which they had founded. According to the Canon of Muratori, Saint John wrote his Gospel at the exhortation of his co-disciples and bishops. Tertullian in the *Adversus Marcionem* writes: "We have Churches which are linked with John. Although Marcion rejects his Apocalypse, the *ordo* of bishops, in its beginning, holds John to be its author." And more amply in the *De prescriptione haereticorum*: "Go through the apostolic Churches, where the see of the apostles still presides in their place. . . . Are you near Achaia? You have Corinth. Are you not far from Macedonia? You have Philippi; you have Thessalonica. If you can go to Asia you have Ephesus. If you are on the borders of Italy you have Rome, whose authority is also at hand for us." In the *Quis dives salvetur*, Clement of Alexandria describes Saint John demanding from one of the bishops whom he had instituted the soul of a young man who had become a brigand leader. All the great Churches preserved episcopal lists that went back to the apostles. Antioch, Alexandria, as well as Rome and Jerusalem knew their first bishops.

Saint Irenaeus, more than any other, is the theologian

of the apostolic succession. For him, the only true and vivifying faith is that which the Church has received from the apostles and which she continues to distribute to her children. For there is to be found in each community the tradition of the doctrine of the apostles authenticated by the present bishops, who go back to the apostles by a continuous and verifiable succession.

These repeated affirmations and this very firm tradition are not without foundation. The bishops are the successors of the apostles. Historically, in certain communities, the college of presbyters may have retained the direction of the Church for a longer time; elsewhere the authority of the bishop, the head of that college, was brought out more quickly.

It is not necessary to admit that the apostles set up bishops everywhere and at the same time, as did Saint Paul, for example, in Crete with Titus. Whilst they were alive they were the heads of the communities. At their death the bishops replaced them. It is clear, therefore, how dangerous it would be to conclude from the silence, even from the complete absence of documents, that the monarchical episcopate was only a later mode of organization. In many Churches—those precisely which we know best— we see it at work before the end of the first century; with regard to the others we have no means of affirming with certitude or of even supposing that it was otherwise.

THE WANDERING PREACHERS

Together with this hierarchy of three degrees, constituted by the bishop, the presbyterium and the deacons, the Didache presents us with a whole series of wandering preachers about whom it supplies some curious information. " Concerning the apostles and the prophets, act thus according to the ordinance of the Gospel. Let every apostle who comes to you be received as the Lord. But let him not stay more than one day, or if need be a second as well.

If he says three days he is a false prophet. And when an
apostle goes forth, let him accept nothing but bread till
he reach his night's lodging; but if he asks for money, he
is a false prophet. Do not test or examine any prophet who
is speaking in the spirit, 'for every sin shall be forgiven,
but that sin shall not be forgiven'. But not everyone who
speaks in spirit is a prophet, except he have the behaviour
of the Lord. From his behaviour, then, the false prophet
and the true prophet shall be known. And any prophet
who, in the spirit, orders a table to be prepared, shall not
eat of it; otherwise he is a false prophet. And every
prophet who teaches the truth, if he do not what he teaches,
is a false prophet."[1]

These preachers assuredly did not form part of the
hierarchy in the strict sense. They come and go from community to community and it is hard to escape the impression that the author of the Didache is suspicious of them.
He does not dare to condemn them because he sees them
as the bearers of the divine Spirit, but he recommends his
readers to prove them according to their behaviour. Doubtless there had been charlatans and deceivers among these
prophets who had succeeded in duping simple folk and
had made themselves at home in the communities, staying
for a long time at their expense. Such disorders must not
be repeated; he who, even in the spirit, demands money for
himself is a false prophet; he does not deserve to be heard.

The stay of the apostles and prophets—these two terms
seem to be, in this case, synonymous—in the Churches they
traversed must be very brief; one or two days only. With
great difficulty permission is granted for them to remain
for a third day, and the faithful are asked to provide them
with the food necessary for them to continue their journey.

It sometimes occurred that the prophets performed
actions or adopted attitudes of such a nature that the faithful were scandalized. "Every prophet who has been tried
and is genuine, and who enacts a cosmic mystery of the

---

[1] Didache xi. 3-10.

F

Church, if he teach not others to do what he does himself, shall not be judged by you; for he has his judgment with God, for so also did the prophets of old."[1] The critics have vainly exercised their ingenuity in trying to discover what this cosmic mystery of the Church could be. It might as well be confessed at once that they have not succeeded in explaining it. It may have been a symbolic action, perhaps analogous to those performed of old by Jeremiah or Ezechiel, and which by its strange character provoked some disturbance in men's minds. Since the authors of those mysteries had already been tried and the authenticity of their mission admitted, they could not further be judged. God alone could do that.

It is hardly probable that the wandering preachers had the right to celebrate the Eucharist. There is indeed mention of tables ordered to be prepared. But this must refer to meals prepared for the poor; the prophets themselves are asked to abstain from them. Then, after the prayers of thanksgiving, of which we have already spoken, the author adds: "Suffer the prophets to make thanksgiving as they will." This is as if the ordinary Christians had to make regular use of the formulae indicated, whilst the prophets, inspired by the Spirit, might prolong their prayers indefinitely. And it is precisely this notification which seems to offer a further proof that the thanksgivings in the Didache refer to ordinary meals and not to the Eucharist. This was reserved to the bishops and deacons. The laity content themselves with receiving it; they do not consecrate it.

Outside the Didache the early Christian documents which mention the prophets are very rare. In the Acts of the Apostles we read of the four daughters of Philip the evangelist who had received the gift of prophecy. They must have lived a long time and left a profound memory behind them. Saint Polycrates of Ephesus and, after him, Gaius of Rome, still recall that they died at Hierapolis and

[1] Didache xi. 11.

that their tomb is preserved there. A papyrus fragment mentions the order of prophets; so also does Serapion of Antioch in a letter to Pontius and to Caricus, at the end of the second century. This would be about all, if Montanism had not arisen about the year 170 to give fresh actuality to the prophets. The attitude then taken by the hierarchic Church, confronted by Montanus and his disciples, is characteristic. The bishops, without condemning prophecy, demanded that it should be controlled and its divine origin seriously established. It was the confirmation of measures indicated by the Didache.

" Teachers "[1] played their part for a longer period; but it seems that they never manifested those rather strange characteristics and disconcerting phenomena which made the prophets startling. At the end of the first century they were lay people without a regular mandate who announced the Gospel here and there, out of zeal and devotion. The Didache shows itself more favourable to them than to the prophets, but it presupposes that their teaching also has been subject to a test. " Whosoever man comes and teaches you all these things aforesaid, receive him. But if the teacher himself be perverted and teach another doctrine to destroy these things, do not listen to him, but if his teaching is for the increase of righteousness and knowledge of the Lord, receive him as the Lord."[2] It considers further, if we understand it aright, that their ministry is no longer indispensable in the organized communities. The bishops and the deacons, it says, also fulfil the office of prophets and doctors; which seems to amount to saying that in the Churches where there are bishops and deacons there is not much left for the teachers to do.

Actually, the teachers continued to carry on their activity in the Church for some time to come. Several of them opened schools like those of the pagan philosophers. They taught their beliefs. Saint Justin in Rome, Tatian and Rhodon are good examples. Others, before setting

---

[1] 1 Cor. xii. 28.   [2] Didache xi. 1-2.

themselves up in a community, travelled about trying to make disciples for the cause of the Saviour. Still others wrote "apologies" and thus made themselves the first defenders of the faith in cultivated circles. The Shepherd of Hermas notices their activity in Rome. But nowhere was their activity more profound than in Alexandria.

To sum up: the Didache leaves us with the impression of a period of transition, such as the apostolic age must have been; and this enables us to accept its testimony in this case, however mysterious it may be on other points.

The Christian communities, provided with a complete hierarchy, became thus more and more numerous. The bishop is the head of each of them, although sometimes his authority is not yet clearly detached from that of the presbyterium which assists him. The deacons collaborate with the presbyterium and concern themselves mainly with works of charity and the material administration of the community. But the evangelization of the world is far from being complete and it is carried on mainly by zealous preachers who come and go, according to the exigencies of their profession, or sometimes according to the impulses of the Spirit. These preachers—apostles, prophets and teachers—make the good news known. Whether they owe their mission to their own zeal, or to a divine inspiration, or even to a definite command of the bishop, their doctrine must be controlled and judged to be in conformity with the orthodox teaching. One does not preach one's own preferences in Christianity; and the preoccupation with purity of doctrine is manifest in all the documents. Similarly, we find in them a concern for order, discipline, obedience to the established authorities. From its beginning Christianity has been the religion of authority: it manifested very clearly its attachment to its traditions and its respect for the hierarchy. While refusing to "extinguish the Spirit", while faithfully welcoming the extraordinary graces granted by God to certain of the faithful, it preferred submission to the rule to the charisms.

CHRISTIAN UNITY

From this time a question arises which only received its full meaning when the last of the apostles had died. How was the unity of faith and of the hierarchy maintained in all the Christian communities? So long as the apostles were alive they supervised and directed the Churches founded by them. They preserved and strengthened the bonds of Christian fraternity. When they had disappeared, who fulfilled their role?

Several times already we have remarked that above the local Churches there was the universal Church. At the end of the first century the feeling of Christian unity is everywhere very strong. It was preserved and developed by travel, by communicating through letters, by personal relationships. All the Churches knew each other. Letters or visits were exchanged from one to the other; and on this point nothing is more significant than the correspondence of Saint Ignatius of Antioch. The coming of the venerable captive was notified to his brethren. When the news was heard of his arrival at Smyrna, the Bishops of Ephesus, Magnesia and Tralles hastened to that town to pay their respects to him. At Troas he was met by two deacons, one from Cilicia, the other from Antioch. He himself wrote letters to the Churches. If he was only able to write six, that was because he was pressed for time; but he wanted to write many more. After a short time all his letters were grouped together. Everyone knew about them and was interested in them. The Church of Philippi asked Polycarp of Smyrna for a complete collection of these letters and the bishop sent them without delay. It is not improbable that other communities also wanted this collection. In any case he knew that it was fairly widespread at the end of the second century.

The example of Saint Ignatius was, doubtless, not an isolated one. In the second century it was to be followed by Saint Denis of Corinth and Saint Serapion of Antioch.

There must have been numerous bishops who had correspondents throughout the whole world. In this way they witnessed to their sense of Christian unity.

THE ROMAN CHURCH

Among the letters of Saint Ignatius, that addressed to the Romans is of particular importance. Elsewhere, the Bishop of Antioch did not hesitate to broadcast his counsels; here he limits himself to formulating his intentions. Circumstances, doubtless, afford an explanation of this difference in attitude. When he wrote to the Churches of Asia, Ignatius was addressing those bishops whom he had seen or whom he himself had visited. He knew their religious and moral situation, and he could recall to their minds the great doctrines of the faith. From the Romans he had only one thing to ask; that they should allow him to pour out his blood for Christ and make no effort to turn him from his torture.

But there is something else. Ignatius feels a quite special veneration for the Church of Rome, and this is manifested by the solemnity of the address which he puts at the head of his letter. " Ignatius who is also called Theophorus to her who has obtained mercy in the greatness of the Most High Father, and of Jesus Christ His only Son; to the Church beloved and enlightened by the will of Him who has willed all things which are, according to the love of Jesus Christ, our God; (to the Church) which also presides in the country of the land of the Romans, worthy of God, worthy of honour, worthy of blessing, worthy of praise, worthy of being heard, worthy in its holiness, and president of love, named after Christ, named after the Father, which also I greet in the name of Jesus Christ, the Son of the Father; to those who are united in every one of His commandments, filled with the grace of God unalterably, and filtered clear from every foreign stain, abundant greeting in Jesus Christ, our God, in blamelessness."

The addresses of the other letters are certainly sumptu-
ous, but this surpasses them by far. Such verbal magnifi-
cence is an indication of the unique respect that Ignatius
felt for the venerable Church of Rome.

But there is more. The other Churches "are" at
Ephesus, Magnesia, Tralles. The Church of Rome "presides in the country of the land of the Romans". These
expressions are singular, and the phrase "in the country
of the land of the Romans" has received the most divergent
interpretations from the critics. We would at least under-
line the fact that the Roman Church presides.

Over what does it preside? A little further on Ignatius
writes that it presides over charity. Harnack interprets
this as meaning that the Roman Church was the most
generous, the most charitable and helpful of the Churches,
and he quotes numerous examples of its munificence. But
it has been observed that the verb *presides* is really explicable only if it has the name of a place or of a collectivity as
its complement. It would seem fitting, therefore, that the
word with which it is here construed should designate a
collectivity and not a virtue. And, *de facto*, elsewhere
Ignatius uses the word charity to express the Church; he
says the charity of the Ephesians when he means the
Church of Ephesus. May we not therefore conclude that
in the address of his letter to the Romans he intended to
signify that the Church of Rome presides over all the
Christian communities, over the universal Church?

The argument is indeed not decisive. But in the body
of the letter we find other indications of the respect in
which Ignatius held the Roman Church. These must be
noted. He apologizes for writing to the Romans: "I do
not give you orders as did Peter and Paul; they were
apostles, I am only a condemned man."[1] Peter and Paul,
therefore, had had personal relations with the Church of
Rome, and on occasions had issued commands to it. We
may see in this an affirmation that Saint Paul had written

[1] Rom. iv. 3.

to the Romans, had come to Rome and died there, and Saint Peter likewise. The authority of the apostles was incommunicable; it belonged to them alone. Ignatius, a captive, condemned to death, could not command as they had done.

Elsewhere Ignatius also declares: "You have taught others. I desire that those things should stand fast which you teach and prescribe."[1] What teachings and prescriptions are referred to here? We cannot say with certainty what are the actions envisaged by the Bishop of Antioch. But it remains that he knew that the Roman Church sent instructions to other Churches and that these had to be followed. The fact is of importance; for it shows the unique place then held by the community of Rome and by its bishop. When the other Churches want to know where the deposit of faith and its discipline is conserved, it is to Rome that they must turn.

We can also quote a case some years previous to the letters of Saint Ignatius in which the Roman primacy is manifestly affirmed. Towards the end of the reign of Domitian troubles had broken out in the Church of Corinth. Certain rash and insolent agitators had stirred up the faithful against their presbyters, so thoroughly and to such effect that the dismissal of several of them had been obtained. We do not know the particular grievances that were alleged. An attempt has been made to interpret it as an episode in the conflict between the inspired prophets and the established hierarchy. There is no reason to believe that this is a sound explanation, for in the document in which the memory of the controversy has been preserved, there is nowhere any question of the charismata. But what is certain is the fact that on hearing of the schism the Roman Church intervened as a duty. Its head, Clement, wrote, in its name, a long letter on peace and concord. This letter is an admirable monument of the Catholic spirit; it commands nothing; it prescribes

[1] Rom. iii. 1.

nothing; it is content to exhort. But its exhortations are sufficiently precise and firm to leave no room for any discussion.

It would be of interest to know whether the Corinthians themselves took recourse to Rome, and solicited its intervention. The texts do not say so; and it is more probable that Clement wrote without having been asked. It is not the only instance, in these early centuries, of a bishop writing to other Churches in order to reprove and correct them. At the time when Soter was the Bishop of Rome (166–175) Saint Denis of Corinth wrote one letter which is a catechesis of orthodoxy and which deals with peace and unity; another to the Athenians on the laxity of their faith; and a third to the Christians of Nicomedia to defend the rule of truth against the heresy of Marcion. Seventy years earlier, Clement, like Denis, is concerned for all the Churches, and tries to maintain everywhere the unity of faith and discipline. But there is something particular in the case of Clement. He is the head of the Roman Church, and that Church already feels itself to be in possession of a superior and exceptional authority which, in the time to come, it will never cease to claim.

Thus even before the end of the first century Christianity has found its centre. It is something quite other than a plurality of Churches, each going its own way and allowing itself to be guided by the chance of circumstances or the inspiration of the Spirit. It is also something quite other than a federation of Churches, trying to keep intact the traditional deposit of the faith and united among themselves by the bonds of charity. It is the Catholic Church; everywhere where there are Christians they are conscious of forming part of a unique body. And this body has one head, which is at Rome. "The faith which is one, as the Lord is one, fashions the scattered Churches and faithful into a still more profound unity, that of the supernatural life which is common to all the faithful in Christ and in the Spirit. The Church, formed of all the Churches, is mystically the body of Christ; and the faithful are individually its members. There is a circumincession of the visible and the invisible. Where the bishop is, *there* is the local Church; just as where the Catholic Church is, *there* is Jesus Christ."[1]

[1] P. Batiffol.

CHAPTER IV

THE JUDAEO-CHRISTIANS AT THE END OF THE FIRST CENTURY

In Palestine. In the Diaspora. The Church of Jerusalem. The Desposynes. The Hebrew Gospel. The Sects.

IN PALESTINE

It was in Palestine that Christianity originated, and the Jewish people were the first to receive the good news. From the day of Pentecost the inhabitants of Jerusalem had Jesus Christ preached to them by the apostles, and those who were converted formed the very earliest nucleus of the whole Christian Church. The rest of Palestine was soon evangelized in its turn; in the *Acts of the Apostles* we read of preachers and faithful in Samaria, at Azotus, Lydda, Joppa, Caesarea and in the plain of Sharon, and the author does not claim to enumerate all the places which the missionaries visited.

Nevertheless it does not seem that Christian propaganda met with great success in Palestine. The Jews as a whole were too proud of the alliance that God had formerly contracted with their fathers, too attached to the hopes of a nationalist Messianism, to accept the preaching of the apostles. The Acts indicate the obstacles which the disciples of Jesus met from the beginning: the imprisonment of Peter, the death of Stephen, the martyrdom of James are the culminating points of an unending and most

varied opposition. Perhaps only the Christian community
of Jerusalem was able to maintain and develop itself,
whilst the other Palestinian Churches vegetated in the
shade without hope and without history.

But even this community at Jerusalem manifested
a dangerous particularism. Most of its members were
recruited from the Jews, and these, as Christians, asserted
that they could not renounce the Mosaic Law. They even
wished that, universally, the newly converted should be
circumcised and keep the Law. The opposition of Saint
Paul to such demands will be recalled. The great apostle
succeeded in gaining his point only after considerable
opposition, as we learn from the Acts of the Apostles.

IN THE DIASPORA

Even outside Palestine this state of mind tended to
develop in certain communities. Almost everywhere the
Gospel had been first announced to the Jews; and although
in general the Jews of the dispersion held to a less rigid
legalism than those of Jerusalem, they were not disposed to
give up Moses. Those who were converted could hardly
help looking at things from the viewpoint of the Law and
thinking of themselves as privileged in relation to their
brethren of pagan origin. The conflicts whose memory has
been kept in the Epistle to the Galatians, were to be
repeated in more or less violent forms in many other
Churches than that of Galatia.

But we have hardly any information about these
Christians of Jewish origin, these Judaeo-Christians who
remained faithful to the circumcision while admitting the
Gospel and recognizing that Jesus was the Messiah. We
nowhere find them founding separate communities and
living apart from the main body of the Church: only from
time to time, at the end of the first century and at the
beginning of the second, we come upon traces of their

activity and note the influence they attempted to exercise here and there.

The letters of Saint Ignatius show them at work in several Churches of Asia Minor. "Be not led astray by strange doctrines or old fables which are profitless," writes the holy bishop to the Magnesians. "For if to-day we live according to Judaism, we should be admitting that we have not received grace. The divine prophets themselves lived according to Jesus Christ; that is why they were persecuted. . . . For whoever adds another name to his own as Christian is not of God. Put aside then the evil leaven, which has grown old and sour, and transform yourselves into the new leaven which is Jesus Christ. . . . It is monstrous to have Jesus Christ on your lips and to practise Judaism. For Christianity did not base its faith on Judaism, but Judaism on Christianity, and the people of every language who believe in God have been brought together in it."[1] The same advice recurs in the letter to the Philadelphians: "If anyone interprets the prophets to you in the sense of Judaism do not listen to him. For it is better to hear Christianity from the circumcised than Judaism from the uncircumcised. But both of them, unless they speak of Jesus Christ, are to me tombstones and sepulchres of the dead, on whom only the names of men are written."[2] In this it is easy to observe the efforts of a clever propaganda which under the cover of the law and the prophets tried to prove the necessity of Judaic observances. Saint Ignatius remains attached to the prophets and declares that they were the first to believe in Jesus Christ. But he is determined to free the faithful from all attachment to Judaism and to proclaim their entire independence of the law.

The unknown author of the letter of Barnabas goes further than Saint Ignatius. He wrote indeed during a period of crisis and had in mind a situation of quite special gravity. He was under the necessity of answering

[1] Magn. viii. and x.   [2] Philad. vi.

a particularly dangerous attack from the Judaizers and of affirming that the Old Testament must be interpreted by the Church in an allegorical sense. His thesis is venturesome; he claims that the Jews have no longer any right to their sacred books, which now belong exclusively to the Church. "And this I ask you again, as being one of yourselves, and especially as loving you all above my own life; take heed to yourselves now, and be not made like unto some, heaping up your sins and saying that the Testament is both theirs and ours. It is ours indeed; but they have lost for ever the testament they received of old from Moses."[1] What was the value therefore of carrying on the practices of Judaism. "The long-suffering God foresaw that the people whom He prepared in His Beloved should believe in guilelessness, and made all things plain to us beforehand that we should not be shipwrecked by conversion to their law. Therefore examining earnestly into present circumstances, we must seek out that which is able to save us. Let us utterly flee from all the works of lawlessness lest they overcome us, and let us hate the error of the present time that we may be loved in that which is to come."[2]

We should like to know exactly to what circumstances and district the principles formulated by the pseudo-Barnabas applied. It is in any case remarkable that these principles still needed to be asserted at the end of the first or, more probably, at the beginning of the second century. By his insistence, the author is an even stronger witness than Saint Ignatius to the existence of an active propaganda in Judaeo-Christian circles.

This propaganda was to show itself at a still later date. In the middle of the second century Saint Justin, who came from Flavia Neapolis in Palestine and who had travelled considerably, declared in his *Dialogue with Trypho* that, in his view, those who, while believing in Christ, had themselves circumcised and kept the provisions

[1] Barn. iv. 6-7.   [2] Barn. iii. 6-iv. 1.

of the Mosaic Law, might be saved, providing they did not attempt to impose this yoke on the Christians converted from heathendom. "There are some," he tells his questioner, "who do not wish even to associate with the faithful who once were pagans, neither in conversation nor at table. If through weakness of spirit they desire to observe as far as they can the practices instituted by Moses, that is understandable on account of the hardness of the people's hearts; and if at the same time they hope in our Christ and observe the eternal principles of justice and natural religion, and if they agree to live with Christians without wanting to impose circumcision, the Sabbath, and other similar practices on them, I declare that we must welcome them and associate with them in all things, as with elder brothers born from the same parents. But if those of your race who say that they believe in Christ use every means to constrain the Gentiles who believe in Christ to live according to the law instituted through the intermediary of Moses, or if they will not agree to associate with them in this same religious life, I shall do as they do and I shall not receive them."[1]

Where did Saint Justin meet these Christians who were still attached to Jewish customs and traditions? He does not tell us, and we cannot know whether it was in Palestine or Ephesus, or even in Rome. At any rate it is important to observe that, during the first half of the second century, Christians were to be found who, while believing in Christ, observed the law of Moses and showed an invincible mistrust towards those believers who came from paganism. By recognizing them as brethren the apologist shows real breadth of mind; he was not only uncertain of his gesture being reciprocated, but he was also aware that he was in some sense in opposition to the majority who would have preferred to leave on one side these backward souls who were powerless to free themselves from the bonds of the law.

A little further on[2] Justin speaks of other Christians

[1] Dial. xlvii. 2-3. [2] Dial. xlviii. 4.

of Jewish origin who admitted that Jesus was the Christ, but who refused to believe in his divinity. "I am not of their opinion," he declares, "nor are the mass of those who are with me." His questioner, on the other hand, is glad to recognize the fidelity of these sections to the Jewish opinions the Messiah. "It seems to me that those who say that he was a man, that he was chosen in order to be anointed, that he was the anointed Christ, affirm something that is more credible than do those who share your opinion. We all of us await a Christ who shall be a man among men, and Elias who must anoint him when he comes."

It seems that it must have been Judaeo-Christians, resembling more or less those whom Saint Justin knew, who first composed and read the pseudo-Clementine apocrypha. The evident hostility to the Apostle Paul, the preponderant place assigned to James, and many other details, are sufficient to show that the original authors— whose works we possess only in a considerably altered condition—lived more or less on the borders of the Orthodox Church, and on many points did not share the ideas of their brethren. The origin of these apocrypha are still too mysterious for them to be utilized here, and, in any case, even in their earliest form they are of too recent a date. But they may be mentioned as marking the persistent vigour of these Christians of Jewish origin and feeling, of whom it is sometimes difficult to say with precision whether they belonged to the Church or depended on the synagogue.

THE CHURCH OF JERUSALEM

Whilst in the communities of the pagan world the Judaeo-Christians carried on their existence in obscurity and without renown, the Church of Jerusalem pursued its venerable career as well as possible. It had been governed for a long while by James who was called the brother of the Lord. Hegesippus, who had collected valuable traditions about him, takes pleasure in recalling the unique veneration in which he was held by all, even by the Jews. " James," he writes, " was sanctified from the womb of his mother. He drank neither wine nor strong drink, and eat nothing that had had life. . . . The skin of his knees had become as hard as that of camels, because he was constantly kneeling, asking pardon for the people. For the rest, his eminent justice led to his being called the Just and Oblias, i.e. 'rampart of the people' and 'justice' in accordance with what the prophets declare about him."[1]

James's holiness, his attachment to the law, his zeal for the traditions of the elders, were unable to save him from the vengeance of the Jews. In the year 62 they took advantage of the death of the procurator Festus and the delay in the arrival of his successor Albinus in order to carry out a surprise attack. During the interval between these two events the priests thought themselves to be the uncontested masters of the situation and consequently dispensed from respect for the law. The high priest of the time was a certain Annas, son of the high priest under whom Jesus had been crucified and a relative of Ananias who had taken part in the trial of Saint Paul. He thought himself sufficiently powerful to have James arrested and brought before the Sanhedrin. The Jewish historian Josephus, a contemporary of the incident, and Hegesippus who lived in the middle of the second century, both wrote a detailed account of this affair, and Eusebius has taken care to transcribe the two texts.[2]

The Pharisees, so it seems, compelled James to go up on a pinnacle of the temple, and asked him to deny Christ. But James, like Stephen, and the other James, the son of Zebedee, refused to perform this act of base desertion. Why, he asked, do you question me about the Son of Man? He is sitting in Heaven, at the right hand of the great power, and He will come again on the clouds of heaven.

[1] Eusebius, H.E. ii. 23, 5-7.   [2] H.E. ii. 23.

G

Many Jews, on hearing these words, were moved to acclaim the Son of David. But the zealots cried out that it was blasphemy. James was thrown from the top of the temple, and since he was not killed by the fall, he was stoned. The generous intervention of a Rechabite was unable to save him; a fuller finished him off by a blow on the head with a stick. He was buried in the place where he fell. At the time of Hegesippus his tombstone was still shown.

It was not long before Annas expiated his crime. Protestations were addressed to the new procurator who arrived from Alexandria, and through him to King Agrippa II. This latter caused the high priest to be deposed and he was replaced by Jesus, the son of Dameas.

Nevertheless the oppression of the Roman domination made itself felt more and more heavily on the Jewish people. Four years after the death of James, in the year 66, under the procurator Gessius Florus, the successor of Albinus, the revolution which had for long been smouldering, broke out in Jerusalem. The magistrate was accused of cruelty; he had inflicted the punishment of scourging on several Jews of distinguished birth; he had even crucified a certain number of zealots. In the autumn the garrison which stayed in the holy city was massacred and the insurrection immediately began. An attempt of Cestius Gallus, the legate of Syria, to retake Jerusalem met with a lamentable setback. The zealots were intoxicated by their success. Even the moderates who had not wanted the war and who did not dare to hope for victory were obliged to allow themselves to be carried away by events, to organize resistance and to join the fanatics. No one listened any longer to the advice which the wise Pharisees and priests still tried to give. The true masters of the situation were the violent and crazy zealots. The most extraordinary prodigies manifested themselves in order to discourage those of good will; but in vain. The movement was irresistible.

In the year 67 Nero had sent Vespasian into Palestine

at the head of an army, and the latter arrived to subdue Galilee. But the troubles which followed the death of the emperor, then the elevation of Vespasian himself to the imperial power, prevented him from carrying out his success. At Jerusalem, the domination of the zealots became more and more tyrannical. Everyone who resisted them was slaughtered without pity. The high priest Ananias himself and his partisans were put to death. Finally, in the year 70, when Vespasian had definitely affirmed his authority, a new army commanded by Titus appeared before Jerusalem and began its siege. The appalling account of the last struggles must be read in Josephus. The defence of the zealots was heroic. In vain the most frightful famine ravaged the population; the resistance went on unbroken. Even after the taking and destruction of the temple in August of the year 70, the citadel still held out. And when in September that was captured, a band of fanatics fled to Mazaba, near the Dead Sea, and held out there for two whole years before being reduced. Nevertheless the taking of Jerusalem and the destruction of the temple by Titus marked the end of the Jewish nation, henceforth deprived of its capital, its sanctuary and its sacrifices.

For the Christians spread throughout the Roman world the event did not have all the importance that one might imagine. For a long time the first converts had kept in constant touch with the mother-community. They had sent alms to it with fidelity. They had felt bound to assure themselves of its approbation. But the bonds had gradually relaxed. After the arrest of Saint Paul, after the death of James, it does not seem that the relations between the Church of Jerusalem and the other Christian communities of the Empire were kept up. How indeed could the Christians have continued to be concerned with a Church that counted so few members and whose tendencies turned more and more away from those which motivated the communities as a whole? It is true that we have very little information about the intimate life of this little Church of Jerusalem during the sorrowful years of the war. If we are to believe Eusebius, who took this information from Hegesippus, " the people of the Church of Jerusalem had received, thanks to a prophecy revealed to the notable men of the place, a warning to leave the town before the war, and to go and live in a certain town of Perea called Pella. It was there that Christ's faithful who left Jerusalem retired. Thus the Jewish metropolis and the whole country of Judaea was entirely abandoned by the saints " before the final ruin.[1] The man who, as head of the community, assumed the responsibility for this exile was Simeon, the son of Clopas who had succeeded James.

The taking of Jerusalem helped to emphasize the antagonism between the Jews and the Christians, even those of Jewish origin. If we are to believe a passage in the Chronicle of Sulpicius Severus that is thought to have been taken from the lost part of the Annals of Tacitus, this antagonism now began to be evident even to the pagans. In a council held on the 9th August of the year 70, Titus asked whether the Temple should be destroyed; several of his officers agreed with him that this destruction was opportune in order to suppress more completely the religion of the Jews and the Christians. " These religions," they added, " although in conflict with each other, have nevertheless the same origins; the Christians have issued from the Jews, and when the root is cut away, its off-shoot will be easily destroyed."

In order to make the separation more complete, the Jews inserted in the prayer that each had to recite three times a day—the *Chemone esre*—a special curse against the Minim. " May the apostates have no hope and may the empire of pride be uprooted promptly in our time. May the Nazarenes and the Minim perish in an instant.

---

[1] Eusebius, H.E. iii. 5, 3.

May they be effaced from the book of life and not counted among the Just. May thou, Jah, who humblest the proud, be blessed." The addition is due to R. Gamaliel II, who invited someone in the assembly to propose a formula, as though it demanded a kind of inspiration. Samuel the Little took on this role about the year A.D. 80.

In several places the Talmud vigorously condemns the Minim, towards whom it displays a particular severity. "If a Gentile or a shepherd or a breeder of small cattle falls into a well, he is left there, but he is not thrown into it. The Minim, the apostates, and the informers are also left there, but they are thrown in as well." Although, *de jure*, this term Minim designated all kinds of heretics, it was, in fact, most commonly applied to Jews who had become Christians, and especially to those who, even after their conversion, did not wish to break entirely with the Law. However late the composition of the Talmud may be, we can be certain that Judaism would never show more sympathy for the Judaeo-Christians than for those of pagan origin and that their secession at the time of the great war did not dispose the rabbis in their favour.

The Christians, on their side, detached themselves more and more from their brethren who accepted the Judaic observances, and quickly forgot the community of Pella. Since the death of James, the brethren of Jerusalem were under the guidance of Simeon, who owed the honour of having received the episcopal see to the fact of being a relative of the Lord. He it was who, after the tragic years of the war, reorganized as well as possible the decimated community at Pella and in other towns of Trans-Jordania. He lived until the reign of Trajan. About the year 107, Atticus being governor of Palestine, he was condemned to be crucified. He was then 120 years old.

Eusebius[1] has preserved for us, probably from the Memoirs of Hegesippus, a long list of the bishops of

---

[1] Eusebius, H.E. iv. 5, 3.

Jerusalem, all of them Hebrews of the old stock as were their flock, who ruled the Church until the time of Hadrian. After James and Simeon come thirteen other names: Justus, Zacchaeus, Tobias, Benjamin, John, Mathias, Philip, Seneca, Justus, Levi, Ephrem, Joseph, Judas. It will be observed that almost all these names have a Hebraic sound, and there is no reason why the others should not have belonged to authentic Jews. We know, however, only the names, and they give rise to more problems than they solve. It is a legitimate matter for surprise to find thirteen bishops succeeding each other so rapidly—perhaps in the course of twenty years—in a single Church. There is nothing theoretically impossible about it, but it is unlikely. It has also been supposed that at least some of these persons lived at the same time and governed other communities than that of Jerusalem —that of Pella, for instance, which doubtless retained both the name and the traditions of Jerusalem.

THE DESPOSYNES

One of the most remarkable characteristics of the Church of Pella—in fact the only one we know—is its fidelity towards the relatives of the Lord or towards those who had some right to claim this title. We have already noted that James and Simeon belonged to the family of Jesus. During the episcopate of Simeon, the Emperor Domitian, anxious about his authority, and always mistrustful of the loyalty of the Jews, one day commanded, as the result of the denunciations of certain heretics, that all the descendants of David should be sought out and put to death. It is not impossible that this order originated in some disturbances of a Messianic nature or at least in a sudden restatement of the ancient prophecies. Hegesippus gives us the curious story of this affair.

" Of the family of the Lord there were still living the

grandchildren of Jude, who was called the Lord's brother according to the flesh. Information was given that they belonged to the family of David, and they were brought to the Emperor Domitian by the Evocatus. For Domitian feared the coming of Christ as Herod also feared it. And he asked them if they were descendants of David, and they confessed that they were. Then he asked them how much property they had and how much money they possessed. And they both of them answered that they had only nine thousand denarii, half of which belonged to each of them; and this property did not consist of silver, but of a piece of land which contained only thirty-nine acres, and from which they raised their taxes and supported themselves by their labour. Then they showed their hands, exhibiting the hardness of their bodies, and the callousness produced upon their hands by continuous toil as evidence of their own labour. And when they were asked concerning Christ and His Kingdom, of what sort it was and when and where it was to appear, they answered that it was not a temporal or an earthly kingdom, but a heavenly and angelic one, which would appear at the end of the world, when He should come in glory to judge the quick and the dead, and to give to everyone according to his works. Upon hearing this, Domitian did not pass judgment against them, but, despising them as of no account, he let them go, and by a decree put a stop to the persecution of the Church. But when they were released they ruled the Churches because they were witnesses (martyrs) and were also relatives of the Lord. And peace being established, they lived until the time of Trajan."[1] For a long time yet the family of the Lord lasted on in Palestine. At the time of Julius Africanus, in the middle of the third century *desposynes* were still to be met with; and they were held in high esteem in Judaeo-Christian circles.

---

[1] Eusebius, H.E. iii. 20, 1-6.

THE HEBREW GOSPEL

The Judaeo-Christians were separated from the main body of the Church by their customs and observances, and also by their language. Everywhere else the faithful spoke Greek and read the Gospels, the letters of Saint Paul and many other writings in Greek. The Judaeo-Christians always used Aramaic and they had a Gospel in this dialect. We have already noticed this *Gospel according to the Hebrews* and sketched briefly some of the problems with regard to its identification. It seems to have been characterized by a definitely anti-Pharisaic tendency and by a firm insistence on the harmony between the two Testaments. As far as one can gather, the personality of James received special emphasis; to him was reserved the first appearance of the risen Christ. Some of the thoughts or phrases which it attributes to the Lord are truly fine and deserve to be remembered. " Never be happy, except when you see your brother in charity." " If you were in my bosom and you did not do the will of my father which is in heaven, I would tear you from my bosom." Only known outside its land of origin by a few specialists, the *Gospel according to the Hebrews* was never very widespread. At the end of the fourth century it was only with difficulty that few copies might be found in libraries or in the last communities that had remained faithful to the Judaeo-Christian tradition.

THE SECTS

The Church of Jerusalem had to endure not only isolation but also heresy; and it was divided into several rival sects. At least Hegesippus assures us that during the episcopate of Simeon, a certain Thebutis, irritated at not having been made bishop, " began among the people the work of corruption which comes from the seven (Jewish) sects to which he himself belonged. From these there came Simon, the head of the Simonians; Cleobius, head of the Cleobians; Dositheus, head of the Dositheans; Gortheus, head of the Gorathenians, and the Masbotheans. After them there appeared the Menandrians, the Marcianists, the Carpocratians, the Valentinians, the Basilidians, the Saturnilians, all of whom introduced, each in its own way, their different particular opinions.[1]

It must be confessed that the good historian is here ill informed. However little we may know of the details of this obscure period, we have no difficulty in correcting him on several points. The Masbotheans, whom he indicates as a Christian sect, reappear a little further on as a Jewish heresy. The Simonians, already mentioned in the Acts of the Apostles, were originally a pre-Christian gnosis. The Gorathenians and the Dositheans are mentioned by Saint Epiphanius as offshoots of the Samaritans, and the illustrious heresiologue himself has little to tell us about them. It seems that all that can be retained with certainty from the fine genealogy of Hegesippus is that towards the end of the second century Palestine was a land of intense syncretism, that the most varied opinions and the most diverse acts found a kind of meeting ground there, and that the purity of its primitive faith was exposed to the worst contaminations.

Hegesippus says nothing of the Ebionites, but later heresiologues give copious information about them. Several of them ascribe their foundation to a certain Ebion, whose existence is at least doubtful. It is probable that their name came from the poverty they practised, the word *ebion* in Hebrew signifying *poor*.

Their doctrine was as follows. They admitted the existence of one only God, the Creator and Master of the world. They declared that Jesus Christ was only a man like other men, and born from Joseph and Mary. "Through his scrupulous observation of the law, Jesus

[1] Eusebius, H.E. iv. 22, 5.

was justified and became Christ. And anyone can become Christ in the same way. The Ebionites kept faithfully all the ordinances of this law and circumcision and the Sabbath. They asserted that this fidelity is necessary to salvation. On the other hand . . . they would have nothing to do with Saint Paul or his Epistles, because they considered him an apostate. But they solemnized Sunday like Christians in memory of the resurrection of Jesus Christ. Saint Irenaeus adds that they explained the prophecies *curiosius*, that is, probably, by mingling rabbinic subtilties or secret traditions with them.''[1]

But in spite of everything, all this remains sufficiently vague. It seems, moreover, that before the end of the first century the Ebionites came into contact with the Essenians, who lived on the borders of the Dead Sea, and borrowed from them a part of their practices and beliefs. The Essenians are known to us chiefly through Philo, Josephus and Pliny the Elder. They were Jews whose main object was purity. To realize this ideal they formed separate communities, whose members—all of whom were celibate—were recruited by adoption or co-optation. Certain of them, it seems reasonable to think, borrowed from the Ebionites their belief in the Messianic character of Jesus; this would be the Essenian Ebionism represented by the Clementine apocrypha which we have already mentioned.

This would be the place to speak of Mandaism, whose first beginnings have certainly nothing in common with Christianity, but which arose in Palestine, and more precisely among the Essenians, towards the commencement of the first century of our era. Unfortunately we know very little about the beginnings of this sect, in spite of the numerous works that have been devoted to it in recent years. We can only ascertain its doctrine from the time when, having borrowed elements from both Judaism and Christianity, it was fixed by writing. It is now certain that

[1] J. Tixeront.

Christianity owes nothing to Mandaism. But one cannot refrain from asking whether the faithful of Palestine did not have the opportunity of observing the Mandeans before these latter finally left Palestine in the reign of Hadrian.

The Helchasaites should also be noticed. We know them chiefly through Hippolytus. They seem to have been closely related to the Mandeans. Saint Epiphanius, who also devotes a chapter to them, relates them to the Ossenians and the Sampseans. He relates that their founder, Elchasai, had joined the former under Trajan, and he gives the name Elchasaites to those whom he also calls Sampseans. All this is not very clear. But at least we can hold that Syria was the land of origin of all these people. The Ossenians came from the country of the Nabateans, Iturea and the Moabitide. Elchasai, after having received a mysterious book from an angel twenty-four schenes (more than eighty miles) high, and four schenes wide, in the third year of the reign of Trajan, i.e. in the year 100, established himself on the banks of the Arnon in order to preach his doctrine. Elchasai attributed the greatest importance to baptism. The sinner who sought pardon must be baptized by him in cold water, in the Name of the Great and Most High God and in the Name of His Son, the Great King, after having called as witnesses heaven, water, the holy spirits, the angels of prayer, oil, salt and the earth, that henceforth he would sin no more, commit no more thefts, adulteries, injustices, acts inspired by cupidity or hatred, perjuries, or any evil action.

His teaching was a strange mixture of Judaism and Christianity. From Judaism he retained circumcision, the observance of the Sabbath and contempt for celibacy. He borrowed belief in Christ from Christianity; but he declared that Christ had been a man like other men, and that he had been incarnate many times previously in the past. He kept a part of the New Testament, the chief thing he rejected being the Epistles of Saint Paul, because he was the apostle of the Gentiles. To all this he added magical superstitions and practices, so that Elchasaism is a veritable mess.

It will be evident from this brief résumé that the religious situation in Palestine and in Trans-Jordania about the year 100 was extremely complex. There were the faithful Jews who wept over the memory of Jerusalem and who tried, in spite of prohibitions, to build up the ruins of their capital. There were the Judaeo-Christians, grouped under the direction of Simeon, who affirmed their fidelity to Jesus Christ, whilst practising the observances of the Mosaic Law. And together with these there fermented numerous sects, more or less related to Judaism and Christianity from whom they had borrowed some elements, but fundamentally pagan from the superstitious practices with which they were encumbered.

None of these sects exercised a real influence on Christianity. Most of them never even left their land of origin, and the only one that has survived all storms up to our own time—Mandaism—owes this extraordinary longevity to the isolation into which its members fled.

The Judaeo-Christians of Palestine remained isolated also. They lived apart from the main body of the Church, without sharing in the great movements of life which animated it. Already few in numbers and without influence at the end of the first century, they were still more weak three centuries later when Saint Jerome visited them. But they still remained faithful to their principles. The great doctor represents them as Christians who lived in the Jewish manner and claimed to observe the law of Moses. Saint Epiphanius, who was equally interested in them and devotes some space to them in his Panarion, gives a similar description. From the time of Saint Paul such an attempt was doomed to failure. It is wonderful that it found propagandists and believers over so long a period.

CHAPTER V

HERESY AT THE END OF THE FIRST CENTURY

The First Heresies. Heresy in Asia Minor at the time of Saint John. Cerinthus. Heresy at the time of Saint Ignatius. Simon.

THE FIRST HERESIES

FROM its origin Christianity has taken the form of an orthodoxy. It has taught a clearly defined doctrine, and put its believers on their guard against all possible deviations from that doctrine. This is a fact of capital importance; the first missionaries ran the risk of often being more zealous than instructed: with the best faith in the world, they might come to preach only their personal opinions and place themselves in disagreement with the authentic teaching of which the apostles were the depositaries. From the time of Saint Paul such a case has been foreseen: "I would that ye knew," the apostle writes to the Colossians, "what great conflict I have for you, and for them at Laodicea, and for as many as have not seen my face in the flesh. I would that your hearts might be comforted, being knit together in love, and endowed with all riches of full assurance of understanding the mystery of God, the Father, and of Christ in whom are hid all the treasures of wisdom and knowledge. And this I say, lest any man should beguile you with enticing words. For though I be absent in the flesh, yet am I with you in the spirit, joying and beholding your order, and the steadfastness of your faith in Christ. As ye have therefore received Jesus Christ the Lord, so walk ye in him; rooted and built up in him, and established in the faith, as ye have been taught, abounding therein in thanksgiving.

"Beware lest any man spoil you through philosophy and vain deceit, after the tradition of men, after the rudiments of the world, and not after Christ. . . . Let no man judge you in meat or in drink, or in respect of feast days, or of the new moon, or of the sabbath days. All these are a shadow of things to come. The reality belongs to Christ. Let no man condemn your efforts, nor humiliate you in the worship of angels, nor impose on you by his visions, vainly puffed up by his fleshy mind, not holding the head from which all the body by joints and bands having nourishment ministered, and knit together, increaseth with the increase of God. Wherefore if ye be dead with Christ from the rudiments of the world, why as though living in the world do ye dogmatize thus: . . . Take not; taste not; touch not even those things which perish with the using? These are the commandments and the doctrines of men, which have indeed a show of wisdom in their system of superstition, abasement of the mind and neglect of the body, but in reality have no value, nothing which does not tend towards the satisfying of the flesh."[1]

Nothing is more expressive than this passage from the Epistle to the Colossians. It is evident that even in the life-time of the apostle the true doctrine was fundamentally attacked by erroneous teaching and that the faithful had to keep themselves on guard against all the heresies preached by false teachers. Saint Paul does not show astonishment at this swarming of error; but he condemns it with all his energy. "There is," he says elsewhere, in the letter to the Ephesians, "one body and one Spirit, as you have been called in our hope of your calling. One Lord, one faith, one baptism. One God and Father of all, and through all, and in us all."[2]

The Pastoral Epistles, written a little later, describe the heresy in more precise terms. The apostle knew its

---

[1] Coloss. ii. 1-8; 16-23. [2] Eph. iv. 4-6.

leaders and he denounces them: Hymenaeus, Alexander the coppersmith, Philetus. He knew that the heretics were recruited from the circumcised, of whom many are " unruly and vain talkers and seducers, whose mouths must be stopped ".[1] He declares that they only seek gain and that under a show of piety they allow themselves to commit all kinds of faults. " They profess that they know God; but in works they deny Him, being abominable and disobedient, and unto every good work reprobate."[2]

The doctrine of these seducers essentially consisted in endless discussions on interminable genealogies and ridiculous stories. They amused themselves with idle questions; they quarrelled over words, over the meaning of the law; they vaunted Jewish fables and human traditions. They forbade certain foods and prohibited marriage. They affirmed that the resurrection had already taken place. In short, we find here a mixture of Judaism and Hellenic speculation. It was already Gnosticism that Saint Paul had to combat.

HERESY IN ASIA MINOR AT THE TIME OF SAINT JOHN

After Saint Paul's death, the heresy he had denounced with so much vigour continued to develop. It seems to have found a particularly favourable soil in the communities of Asia Minor, where we had already observed its manifestation at Colosse, Laodicea, and Ephesus. The seven letters to the Churches of Asia in the Apocalypse of Saint John throw a strong light on the rapid and crafty propaganda of the teachers of falsehood. Asia Minor had always been the promised land of syncretism; its old indigenous religions had become associated with the worship of the deities of Olympus; and when the adoration of the Emperors became fashionable, it was nowhere more welcomed than in these regions. Christianity pro-

[1] Tit. i. 10-11.   [2] Tit. i. 15-16.

claimed the nothingness of the idols and the vanity of the false gods; but too often it was only superimposed upon the beliefs and cults it came to destroy. Almost everywhere Saint John was obliged to condemn the errors into which large numbers of the faithful kept falling. " I have a few things against thee," he declares to the Church of Pergamos, " because thou hast there them that hold the doctrine of Balaam, who taught Balac to cast a stumbling-block before the children of Israel, making them eat things sacrificed unto idols and to commit fornication. So hast thou also them that hold the doctrines of the Nicolaitanes."[1] Similarly to the Church of Thyatira: " I have a few things against thee because thou sufferest that woman Jezebel, which calleth herself a prophetess, to teach and to seduce my servants to commit fornication and to eat things sacrificed unto idols."[2] Elsewhere, at Ephesus, Sardis and Laodicea, Saint John denounces similar disorders. Out of the Seven Churches whom he addresses, those of Smyrna and Philadelphia alone have merited unqualified praise from him.

The error, as it appears from these texts, first of all takes the form of a moral disorder: it authorized all kinds of faults against purity and was indulgent towards the worst excesses. But it did not stop there; for its culpable practices were justified by their propagators in the name of a doctrine which the apostle stigmatizes by calling it the depths of Satan.

The Apocalypse does not enter into further details; but we learn from it that the heretics of Asia were called Nicolaitanes and a later tradition provides more information about them. Saint Irenaeus and Saint Hippolytus refer this name of Nicolaitanes to one of the seven deacons mentioned in the Acts: Nicolas, a proselyte of Antioch; we do not know on what tradition they rely for this. Clement of Alexandria, while agreeing that it was from Nicolas that the sect derived its name, exculpates him from all

---

[1] Apoc. ii. 14-15.   [2] Ibid. 20

personal error. Nicolas, he says, had a woman of whom
he was extraordinarily enamoured. The apostles having
reproached him about her, he brought her into the
assembly and allowed her to be taken by whoever wanted
her. He was afterwards married and had a son who lived
an exemplary life and some daughters who remained
virgins. His maxim was that the flesh should be maltreated
—words that for him had an ascetic meaning, but his
disciples understood otherwise, seeing in them an en-
couragement to immorality.

CERINTHUS

The Nicolaitanes were not the only heretics with which
Saint John had to be concerned. According to a tradition
by Saint Irenaeus, the apostle wrote his Gospel expressly
to combat the errors of Cerinthus. The latter must have
lived at Ephesus, and Saint Polycarp relates that one day
when Saint John had gone into the baths he observed
Cerinthus there, and ran out crying: "Fly; the house may
fall down for it is sheltering Cerinthus, the enemy of
truth."

The teaching of Cerinthus is known to us, thanks
mainly to Saint Irenaeus and to the Roman priest Caius
who lived at the beginning of the third century. According to Saint Irenaeus, the heresiarch taught the distinction
between the supreme God and the demiurge; the power
who created the world is one being, the supreme God
another. Jesus, the son of Mary and Joseph, was a man
just like other men upon whom a power, coming from the
supreme God, had descended the day of his baptism. This
power abandoned him before his Passion and he suffered
and died as an ordinary man. Caius's account is different;
according to him, "Cerinthus by means of revelations set
down as written by a great apostle, presents us, in a lying
manner, with accounts of marvellous things supposed to
have been shown to him by the angels. He says that after

H

the resurrection the reign of Christ will be on earth, that the flesh shall live again at Jerusalem and serve the passions and pleasures. He is an enemy of the divine Scriptures, and as he wishes to deceive men, he says there will be a thousand years of nuptial feasts."[1]

These two accounts are not contradictory; they complete each other. Thanks to them we can see that Cerinthus, while recognizing the supernatural activities of Christ, explained them by the fact that a divine power had descended upon him; but he refused to admit the Saviour's divinity and rejected his virgin birth in consequence. His messianism was entirely national and carnal; it rested upon the expectation of the reign of a thousand years and of the heavenly Jerusalem. The dualism professed by this heretic foreshadows the Gnostic theses which were to attain their complete development in the course of the second century; unlike the other elements of his doctrine, this was obviously not of Judaic origin, but was connected in numerous ways with the ideas of all those who condemned matter and could not persuade themselves that it was the creation of the supreme God.

The ancient authors say nothing about the morality of Cerinthus. Filastrius and Saint Epiphanius represent him as definitely Judaizing: he admitted the Law in part, circumcision and the Sabbath. He therefore rejected the Epistles of Saint Paul and the Acts of the Apostles, and of the Gospels he retained only that of Saint Matthew, but without its genealogy of the Saviour.

Reading the first Epistle of Saint John in the light of the information supplied by Saint Irenaeus and Caius, one can make a better estimate of the gravity of the danger against which the aged apostle had to fight. The Epistle is full of warnings and reminders. The adversaries are not named, but they are felt to be active and menacing. "Who is a liar if not he that denieth that Jesus is the Christ? He that denieth the Father and the Son is an antichrist. Who-

[1] Eusebius, H.E. iii. 28, 1-2.

soever denieth the Son, the same hath not the Father:
he that acknowledgeth the Son hath the Father also."[1]
"Beloved, believe not every spirit, but try the spirits to
see whether they are of God: Because many false prophets
are gone out into the world.   This is how you recognize
the spirit of God: every spirit that confesseth that Jesus
Christ is come in the flesh is of God: and every spirit that
confesseth not that Jesus Christ is come in the flesh is not
of God: and this is that spirit of Antichrist, whereof ye
have heard that it should come: and even now already is
it in the world."[2]

These counsels are repeated right through the Epistle.
The error envisaged by Saint John is an attack on the
person of Christ: it rejected the Saviour's divinity, and it
was to answer it that from the very first lines of his Gospel
Saint John declares: "In the beginning was the Word and
the Word was in God and the Word was God."   Many false
believers imagined that Jesus was nothing else than a man.
Others seem to have claimed that Christ took on only the
appearance of a body.   In reality, "the Word was made
flesh and dwelt among us".

HERESY ACCORDING TO SAINT IGNATIUS

Some years later when Saint Ignatius journeyed across
the province of Asia in order to go to Rome, the situation
had hardly changed.   The heretics were as bold as ever;
they travelled through the communities of Asia Minor in
order to spread their doctrines; they gave frequent lectures
and exhortations in order to combat orthodoxy. At Ephesus
it seems that they obtained no success. But at Philadelphia
the Bishop of Antioch came up against them and had to
discuss their theories at length.

"While I was with you," he writes, "I cried out, I
spoke with a great voice—with God's own voice: 'Give
heed to the bishop, and to the presbytery and to the

[1] 1 John ii. 22-23.   [2] 1 John iv. 1-3.

deacons. But some suspected me of saying this because I had previous knowledge of the division of persons. But He in whom I am bound is my witness that I had no knowledge of this from any human being, but the Spirit was preaching and saying this: Do nothing without the bishop . . . I beseech you to do nothing in factiousness, but after the teaching of Christ. For I heard some men saying: 'If I find it not in the archives, in the Gospel, I do not believe.' And when I said to them that it is in the Scripture, they answered me: 'that is exactly the question.'"[1]

This text is characteristic. The discussion started from the Gospel which the heretics professed to treat as the supreme authority and in which they thought the decisive proof of their doctrine could be found. Ignatius was thus confronted by Christians who admitted the testimony of Scripture. He admitted it also; but he did not find in it the things his adversaries discovered. The controversy might have gone on indefinitely, if Ignatius had not, in the end, appealed to the living tradition, to the bishop and his presbyterium.

These teachers, however, against whom the Bishop of Antioch had to fight, did not teach exactly the same doctrine as the adversaries of Saint John. They claimed that Christ had not taken a body, and that He endured only an appearance of suffering: hence the name of Docetists by which they are known to history. According to them, Christ was indeed the Son of God, but He was not truly a man, for His humanity was only a vain illusion. Saint Ignatius could not warn his correspondents too urgently against their seductions: " For these men, in order to win confidence, mingle Jesus Christ with their errors, mixing as it were a deadly poison with honeyed wine, which the ignorant takes gladly in his baneful pleasure, and it is his death. Be deaf therefore when anyone does not speak to you of Jesus Christ, the descendant of David, born of Mary,

[1] Philad. vii. viii.

who was truly born, both ate and drank, was truly persecuted under Pontius Pilate, was truly crucified and died
in the sight of those in heaven and on earth and under the
earth; who was also truly raised from the dead, when His
Father raised him up, as in the same manner His Father
shall raise up in Christ Jesus us who believe in Him, without whom we have no true life. But if His suffering was
only a semblance, why am I a prisoner, and why do I even
long to fight with the beasts. In that case I am dying in
vain. Then indeed am I lying concerning the Lord."[1]

He repeats the same teaching to the Smyrnaeans.
"You are full believers in the Lord, who is truly of the
race of David according to the flesh, Son of God by the
will and power of God, truly born of a virgin, baptized
by John that all righteousness might be fulfilled by
Him, truly nailed (to the cross) under Pontius Pilate and
Herod the tetrarch, in the flesh for our sakes. . . . For
He suffered all these things for us that we might attain
salvation; and He truly suffered even as He also truly
raised Himself; He did not as some unbelievers assert,
merely suffer in semblance; it is they who are merely in
semblance."[2] A little further on he adds: "There are
some who deny Him through ignorance, or rather, are
denied by Him, being advocates of death rather than of
truth. These are they whom neither the prophecies, nor
the law of Moses persuaded, nor up-to-now even the Gospel,
nor our own individual sufferings. For they have the same
opinion concerning us as concerning him. For what does
anyone profit me if he praise me but blaspheme my Lord,
and does not confess that he was clothed in flesh."[3]

It is particularly the letters to the Trallians and the
Smyrnaeans that define the Docetic character of the heretical Christology. In the other letters, especially in those
to the Magnesians and Philadelphians, Ignatius insists
more on the dangers which the Church might incur from
the observance of Judaic precepts. He condemns those

[1] Trall. vi. 9-10.   [2] Smyrn. 1-2.   [3] Smyrn. v.

who impose circumcision and the rites of Moses upon Christians. No doubt speculations analogous to those formerly denounced by Saint Paul in his letter to the Colossians were mingled with these ritual prescriptions; but Saint Ignatius does not elaborate this point. It is often said that he was dealing with only one heresy characterized by both a Docetic Christology and a superannuated attachment to Jewish observances. This conclusion is not certain; and it is more probable that in reality he was opposing two distinct errors which did not manifest themselves in the same Churches; Docetism on the one hand, and Judaism on the other.

Saint Ignatius hardly mentions the moral life of the heretics. He contents himself with saying that they had no charity towards the poor and indigent, and that they were incorrigible instigators of coteries and schisms. He treats them as specious wolves who capture the faithful by evil pleasures;[1] and he recommends these latter to " keep their flesh as the temple of God ".[2] These remarks are too general to allow us to affirm the immorality of the heretics.

Are there any other evidences of Docetism at the beginning of the second century apart from the Epistles of Saint Ignatius? Certain passages of the Odes of Solomon have been interpreted, as we observed above, as Docetic affirmations; the following, for example:

" She (the virgin mother) became pregnant and
        brought forth a son without pain;
And in order to avoid everything useless, she did
        not ask for a midwife to assist her;
She brought forth voluntarily a semblance of man;
She brought him forth in likeness;
She possessed him in power;
And loved him in salvation;
And kept him in sweetness;
And showed him in greatness."[3]

[1] Philad. ii. 1.   [2] Philad. viii. 2.   [3] Od. xix. 7-10.

This and similar texts are not decisive. Here, especially, it is a question of bringing into emphasis the virgin birth of the Saviour, and it would be wrong to stress unduly words such as semblance and likeness, whose exact interpretation depends on the context. We will only remark that Docetism has been one of the great temptations of Christianity from its very beginning. For to claim that Christ had nothing of man and his infirmities save the appearances, is in reality to do away with Him.

SIMON

There is no other contemporary evidence about heresy at the beginning of the second century. But we know from elsewhere that the activities of the sects were not limited to the forms already described.

The Acts of the Apostles introduce us to a personage called Simon who carried on his activity in Samaria about the years 33–36. Simon was a magician. "He claimed to be someone great. To whom they all gave heed, from the least to the greatest, saying: this man is the great power of God."[1] The preaching of Philip seems to have moved him so that he believed and was baptized. But his intentions were not pure; he claimed the power of working miracles and even offered to buy it for money; for which request he received a terrible rebuke from Peter and John.

It will be seen from this account that Simon's preaching was anterior in origin to Christianity. Thus the doctrine taught by the magician had nothing Christian about it; it was a gnosis resting on pagan myths and magic. Saint Justin, who came from Nablous in Samaria, and who asserts that in his time, about A.D. 150, all the Samaritans venerated Simon as the first God, provides the following information about him: Having bought a public woman, called Helen, who was a prostitute at Tyre, Simon travelled through the country with her. He said that she was his

[1] Acts viii. 10.

thought through whom he had created the angels. This thought having descended from heaven, the angels who had created the world fell in love with her, and on her account waged war. As they kept her prisoner and prevented her from going back to heaven, she passed from one woman's body to another: in particular it was she who was incarnate in the renowned Helen—the occasion of the Trojan War, and incarnate again in the prostitute of Tyre of whom Simon declared: it is for her sake that I have descended; she is the lost sheep whom I must find in order to free her from her bonds and to procure the salvation of men through my knowledge.

The account of the Acts is evidence that Simon soon entered into relations with Christianity. It was not long before a legend grew up making him oppose Saint Peter in scenes of dramatic controversy; it is to be found in the Clementine apocrypha.

But although the later developments of the legend can be neglected, it is probable that the person of Jesus held an important place in the teaching of the Simonites. According to Saint Irenaeus, who doubtless utilized the most ancient sources, the Supreme Power who manifested himself in Samaria as Father in Simon, showed himself to the Jews as Son in Jesus, and in other countries as the Holy Spirit.

Saint Hippolytus, in the Philosophoumena, copies Saint Irenaeus; but he also gives an account of the Simonite theology from a book that seems to have been called *The Great Revelation*. There is an infinite power, an immutable personage, identified with Simon, and then the six principles of things grouped in pairs. But it is very obscure, and there is no need to try to work out the details.

At what precise moment did Simonism agree to accept the person of Jesus among its company? It is impossible to say. It is also impossible to judge the success of its propaganda. Saint Justin, who is the first to inform us that Simon came to Rome in the reign of Claudius Caesar, is certainly mistaken when he speaks of a statue erected to him on an island in the Tiber, with the inscription *Simoni deo sancto.* Can we even be confident that the magician did travel to the capital?

Saint Justin also tells us the name of another teacher of falsehood, Menander, also a Samaritan, from the town of Capparete, and a disciple of Simon. "With the assistance of demons," writes the Apologist, "he deceived many of the inhabitants of Antioch by the prestige of his magic, and made his adepts believe that they would not die; even to-day disciples who believe in him are still to be found."[1] We know nothing else about Menander, and his preaching cannot have had much success. Saint Ignatius does not make the slightest allusion to it, and it seems that after the beginning of the second century, his disciples exercised no influence over the Christians of Antioch.

It is true that neither does the Bishop of Antioch make mention of Satornil, who must have been his contemporary and who was active in Syria. But it is very possible that Satornil, whose disciples are noticed by Saint Justin and Hegesippus, only began his preaching after the death of Ignatius. Our most definite information about him, and that is not very clear, comes from Saint Irenaeus, who seems to make Satornil the first of the great Gnostics.

Satornil taught the existence of a Father God whom no one can name or know, and who created the angels. The world is the work of the seven angels who also made man. The unnameable God has sent to man a spark of life that must be liberated from matter. The God of the Jews is one of the creator angels. Since these have revolted against God, the Saviour came to destroy their power, and especially to conquer the God of the Jews. The Saviour was man only in appearance, but this did not prevent him from accomplishing his work when it came to liberating the spark of life which men, or at least some of them, possessed. Saint Irenaeus's account is not always precise. But one can

[1] 1 Apol. xxvi. 4.

see that the system of Satornil is more simple than that of the later Gnostics. It must have flourished during the first quarter of the second century.

The names and facts that have just been mentioned certainly do not represent all the manifestations of heresy at the end of the first century. The entire East, and more especially Syria, was the scene at that time of an extraordinary throng of sects of every kind. The strangest doctrines encountered each other there, and combined into various syncretisms. It was natural that Christianity, when occasion served, should have provided some of the ingredients for these unexpected mixtures. It was doubtless more protected than most of the other doctrines by the stability of its dogma of monotheism, which was its assured departure point, and also by the historical fact of Christ who, having been really born, really suffered under Pontius Pilate, really resurrected, could not be confused with any of the divinities who shared the adoration of the initiates of the multifarious mystery cults.

But it was impossible to prevent some out of all those who heard the Christian preaching from taking hold of the person of Jesus and of the theme of redemption in order to introduce them, in one form or another, into a new system. In its origin Gnosticism was no more Christian than Simonism: it became so when it accorded a place to Jesus.

If there is something remarkable in the confusion of sects and the medley of ideas, of which our documents only give us an attenuated idea, it is the fact that Christianity did not then succumb; that it kept not only its originality but its already traditional doctrine, and that it maintained it from one end of the world to the other. When the letters of Saint Ignatius speak of Christianity as a definite unity, when they ascribe the name Catholic to the Church, they are the expressions of a fact that perhaps we do not always sufficiently admire. Within each community unity was maintained by the cohesion between the faithful and the hierarchy: those who did not obey the bishop ceased to belong to the Church. Between the different communities of the world there was hardly any other visible bond than that which was created by prayers, letters, visits and alms. But this bond was sufficient. From one end of the universe to the other there was only one Church alone, the body of Christ.

CHAPTER VI

CHRISTIANITY AND THE ROMAN EMPIRE AT THE END OF THE FIRST CENTURY

The Persecution of Nero. The Edict of Nero. Trajan's letter to Pliny. The Persecution of Domitian. Under Trajan.

THE PERSECUTION OF NERO

IT seems to have been in the reign of Nero, and about the year 64, that the Roman Empire began to distinguish Christianity plainly from Judaism and to take up a hostile attitude towards it. Up to that time the two religions had been more or less confused by those in power. About the year 51 or 52, according to historian Suetonius, the Emperor Claudius drove out of Rome Jews who, under the impulse of Chrestus, had caused violent disturbances; and it is generally admitted that the imperial edict was provoked by controversies or riots that had broken out within the Jewish communities of Rome on the subject of Christ. Doubtless, it is not absolutely impossible that an agitator with the name of Chrestus was the cause of the trouble. But this hypothesis is seen to be at least needless from all that we know about the reactions produced in the synagogues by the Christian preaching. Everywhere, the teaching of the apostles had stirred up men's minds and divided the Jewish communities. It was natural the same thing should have happened in Rome.

About the same time, at Corinth, the proconsul Gallio had had to deal with Saint Paul before his tribunal. It was the Jews who had brought the apostle to him, under the pretext that he was teaching a worship contrary to that allowed by the law. To this accusation Gallio was content to answer: "If it were a matter of wrong or a crime, O ye Jews, I would naturally support you. But since it is a question of words and names and of your law, it is for you to see to it. For I will be no judge to such matters."[1] The proconsul's attitude was clear. If he refused to intervene, it was because, in his eyes, the preaching of Saint Paul was only a more or less orthodox form of Judaism.

A little later, the high priest Ananias himself had not yet come to see clearly the difference between Judaism and Christianity. When he presented Saint Paul to the pro-curator Felix, he accused him of being a public nuisance, a mover of sedition, the leader of the heresy of the Nazarenes.[2] In his eyes, Christianity was still only a Jewish sect.

After having been thus prolonged for about thirty years, this confusion between the two religions disappeared. "On July the 19th in the year 64," says Batiffol, "a conflagra-tion broke out in the neighbourhood of the great circus in Rome; in six days and seven nights the fire laid waste the Velabrum, the forum and a part of the Palatine. It burst out again at the other end of Rome, and for three days ravaged the Quirinal, the Vuirinal and the field of Mars. Altogether, out of the fourteen districts of the city, only four were spared, those among others (the Porta Capena and the Trastavere) where the Jews were most numerous. The terrified inhabitants accused Nero of having set fire to Rome so that he could alter its plan according to his own ideas. In order to quieten these rumours Nero put forward other culprits and inflicted the most refined tor-tures upon a class of men detested for their abominations and who were called Christians by the populace."

We know this frightful story from Tacitus. At first

[1] Acts xviii. 14-15.   [2] Acts xxiv. 5.

only a few Christians were apprehended, and these made no difficulty about admitting their belief; then, on their denunciations, an immense multitude were soon arrested; their conviction was based far more on their hatred of the human race than on the burning of the city.

The number of victims was enormous. The Church of Rome long retained the memory of the Neronian persecution, and in his letter to the Corinthians, Clement still alludes to it. "But to cease from the examples of old time, let us come to the athletes who are near to us; let us take the noble examples of our own generation. Through jealousy and envy the greatest and most righteous pillars of the Church were persecuted and contended unto death. Let us set before our eyes the good apostles. Peter, who because of unrighteous jealousy suffered not one or two but many trials, and having thus accomplished his martyrdom, went to the glorious place which was his due. Through jealousy and strife Paul showed the way to the prize of endurance. Seven times he was in bonds, he was exiled, he was stoned; he was a herald both in the East and in the West; he gained the noble fame of his faith. He taught righteousness to all the world, and when he had reached the limits of the West he consummated his martyrdom before the rulers, and thus passed from the world and was taken up into the Holy Place—the greatest example of endurance.

"To these men with their holy lives was gathered a great multitude of the chosen, who were the victims of jealousy and offered among us the finest example in their endurance under many indignities and tortures. Through jealousy women were persecuted as Danaïds and Dircae, suffering terrible and unholy indignities; they steadfastly finished the course of faith, and received a noble reward, weak in the body though they were."[1]

Reading these strong words, one can estimate how great

1 1 Clem. v. vi.

the Neronian persecution had been for the Roman Church. After thirty years it was still thought of as quite a recent event; and those whose memory was thus preserved were not only the two apostles, Peter and Paul, but the immense crowd of every age and of both sexes who had been struck down by the edict of Nero.

THE EDICT OF NERO

For it seems, indeed, that although the fire was the first pretext for the persecution, the emperor afterwards sought to legitimize his conduct by forbidding the profession of Christianity under the most severe penalties. At any rate, the memory of an official act of Nero which condemned the Christian name persisted for a long time. Tertullian, who wrote in the last years of the second century, mentions this *institutum neronianum*, this law, this decree which survived its author in spite of the passing of all his other acts. "Consult your own records," he writes in his Apology. "There you will find that Nero was the first who raged with the imperial sword against this sect, just when it was coming into notice at Rome." And in his book to the nations: "Under the rule of Augustus this name arose. Under Tiberius its discipline shone out for the first time. Under Nero condemnation was brought against it. What we are, the edict showed. But after the abolition of his other acts, this one law of Nero remained."

The statements of Tertullian are clear. They seem to be confirmed by a passage of Suetonius which enumerates a certain number of measures taken by the Emperor Nero; amidst laws on luxury taverns, chariot racing, mimes and forgers, there is an indication of a law against the Christians. "The sale of cooked viands in the taverns was forbidden, whereas before every sort of dainty was exposed for sale. Punishment was inflicted on the Christians, a class of men given to a new and mischievous superstition. He put an end to the diversions of the chariot drivers. . . ."[1] The obvious disorder of this list is a guarantee of its authenticity. The historian must have copied out a kind of table of contents in which the acts of Nero were given chronologically. Who knows whether he was struck by the disproportion between the prohibition of the fooleries of the charioteers and the unqualified condemnation of the Christians?

A more precise testimony is afforded by the first letter of Saint Peter. "Let none of you," writes the apostle, "suffer as a murderer, or as a thief, or as an evildoer, or as a busybody in other men's matters. But if any man suffer as a Christian, let him not be ashamed."[2] The sufferings here envisaged by the apostle are such as might be incurred from the authorities appointed for the repression of thieves, assassins, etc., i.e. from the regular tribunals. It is natural to think that these words were not written before those tribunals had begun to act expressly against the Christians.

Nero's prohibition remained practically a dead letter. At any rate we have no certain evidence of any martyr outside Rome at this time. Even in Rome the persecution was of short duration. Nero had had no time to pursue those Christians who had been able to survive his threats and who had concealed themselves as well as possible. After him, the first Flavians also had sufficient to do, without bothering themselves about the juridical situation of the faithful.

It has been remarked, and the point must be insisted upon, that Christianity was irreconcilable with contemporary ideas to as great an extent as it was with Roman legislation on religious matters. The ancient world admitted neither freedom of worship nor atheism. All men were bound to have one belief and to practise one worship. Naturally, this belief and this worship were those of the nation to which one belonged; and since the gods of poly-

[1] Vita Neronis. xvi. 2.   [2] 1 Peter iv. 15.

theism were not jealous of each other, their clients, having
paid their homage to one set, might go and adore another.
In fact, syncretism was inevitable for anyone who, while
retaining the gods of his own country, wished to adore
those of Rome. The Jews alone refused all compromise.
Attached exclusively to Jahweh, they could not sacrifice
to idols. But no one thought of asking them to, because
Jahweh was their own god, the god of their race and
nation, and while remaining faithful to him, they con-
formed, after all, to the regulations in force. It might have
been feared that after the taking of Jerusalem and the
destruction of the temple, the Jews, having ceased to have
a national existence, would also have been compelled to
renounce Jahweh their God. In reality their privileges
were of too long standing for the events of the year 70 to
have brought any change at all in their legal condition.
Jewish communities existed in every part of the Roman
Empire. Their members met together to pray in the
synagogues; and they made clear their loyalty to existing
institutions. The ruin of the Jewish state left these communities intact; and they kept their rights. Even when
they were dispersed, the Jews constituted a people.

It was not at all the same with the Christians. Their
proselytism broke through all barriers: they addressed
themselves to everyone. And when they had made a conquest, the new believers were obliged to break with their
past, to deny the gods whom up to then they had adored,
to consecrate themselves exclusively to one God alone.
This was practical atheism, with all the religious and social
consequences that the word entailed; being put outside the
law, rupture with the natural institutions and law, i.e. a
state of violence, which could only be punished by capital
punishment.

I

TRAJAN'S LETTER TO PLINY

The best proof of this state of mind is to be found in the answer of the Emperor Trajan to Pliny the Younger, governor of the province of Bithynia from 111–113. We have already read the letter addressed to the Emperor by this honest functionary. That letter leaves no doubt as to the legal situation of the Christians at that time: when Pliny wrote, the mere profession of Christianity was a capital crime: "This is the course I have taken with those who were accused before me as Christians. I asked them whether they were Christians, and if they confessed, I asked them a second and third time with threats of punishment. If they kept to it, I ordered them for execution. . . ." Why? For what crime? Simply because it was a question of a wicked superstition, carried to great lengths. It is true that a great number of the Christians troubled Pliny; they were too many; and if all of them must be put to death, was there not a risk that the province would be decimated? Besides, what exactly ought to be punished? Was it the name itself? Or the crimes connected with the name? This question was of importance when it came to settling the fate of the apostates. For since they had renounced it, they escaped punishment if it was the name that was to be punished. But they continued to deserve it if it was the crimes covered by the name that must be dealt with. One thing at any rate is clear; the necessity of putting this question is evidence that the law had made no precisions about it. It confined itself to striking down Christians as such.

Trajan's answer could not be clearer. "You have followed, my dear Secundus, the process you should have done in examining the cases of those who were accused to you as Christians. For no hard and fast rule can be laid down to meet a question of such wide extent. The Christians are not to be sought out; but if they are accused and convicted, they must be punished, but with this reservation, that if anyone denies that he is a Christian, and makes it clear that he is not, by worshipping our gods, then he is to be pardoned because of his recantation, however suspicious his past conduct may have been."

Trajan tried to soften the law, not in its terms, but in its application. Like Pliny, he was moved by the great number of deaths that were inevitable if all the Christians, irrespectively, were sent to execution. That is why he forbade them to be sought out. Christians were not to be sought out; it was sufficient to punish those who were accused and convicted. "O strange and necessarily illogical sentence," writes Tertullian. "It says that they must not be sought out, as though they were innocent; and it commands them to be punished as though they were criminals. It spares and it acts with cruelty; it shuts its eyes and it punishes. Why expose yourself to blame? If you condemn them, why do you not also seek them out? If you do not seek them out, why do you not also absolve them? For the seeking out of brigands there is a military detachment in each province, designed by lot. Against those guilty of treason and public enemies, every man is a soldier, and the search extends to accomplices and confidants. Only the Christian is not allowed to be sought out, but it is allowed for him to be denounced to the judge, as if the search had any other object than that of denunciation to the judge. You thus condemn a man who has been denounced, although no one has wanted him to have been sought out."

It could not be put better. Trajan's rescript was an abuse of logic. At the same time as he recalls the law that they must be punished, he limits the application—they must not be sought out. The profession of Christianity was theoretically irreconcilable with the essential principles of ancient law: in actual fact, it was tolerated, because it was scarcely possible to do otherwise.

THE PERSECUTION OF DOMITIAN

Between the reigns of Nero and that of Trajan it had been tolerated; and except for a short and violent persecution towards the end of the reign of Domitian, it seems that no serious obstacle had arisen to disturb the peace of the Church. We are not well informed about Domitian's persecution, in spite of the fact that Clement's letter to the Corinthians was written immediately after it, and that it briefly recalls the sudden misfortunes and calamities which, one after another, fall upon the Roman community. It has been supposed that the fiscal measures taken by the Emperor against the Jews—he had exacted the payment of the didrachma from all those who lived as Jews—had rebounded on the Christians, who, in certain circles, were still barely distinguished from the Jews, and that this operation, carried through with rigour, naturally produced its victims. That is possible. But account must also be taken of Domitian's personal disposition; for he was, on principle, most attached to Roman traditions and hostile to any novelty.

In any case, the only Roman martyrs of this period that are known to us were put to death under the two-fold pretext of atheism and a Jewish mode of life. The most celebrated of them were the consul Clement and his wife Flavia Domitilla. Clement was executed in the year 95, the very year of his consulate. Flavia Domitilla was exiled to the island of Pandataria. Another Flavia Domitilla, their niece, was sent to the island of Pontia. Later on, legend took hold of these personages whose noble birth and dignity of life had made them particularly prominent. In the fourth century the Acts of Saints Nereus and Achilleus supplied all kinds of details about their actions, their companions and the manner of their death, which have not the least historical value. The two sons of Clement, who had received from the Emperor the names of Vespasian and Domitian, and whom he had destined to be his successors on the throne, do not seem to have been molested. But the death of Domitian put an end to the imperial destiny of the Flavian family.

Many other Christians of Rome were also the victims of Domitian. Among them is mentioned the consul Acilius Glabrion, who was accused of being a revolutionary, *molitor novarum rerum.* Dion Cassius and Eusebius affirm that the numbers of martyrs was considerable, and indeed, Clement's letter gives the impression of having been written on the morrow of a brief but extremely grievous storm.

It seems also that the persecution was not limited to the city of Rome. There is the tradition, recorded by Tertullian, according to which the aged apostle John was brought to the capital and there plunged into boiling oil. He came out healthier and stronger than when he went in. The Apocalypse, on the other hand, informs us that John was exiled to the island of Patmos, " For the word of God and for the testimony of Jesus Christ."[1] This suffering may be dated before or after his suffering at the Latin Gate.

The Apocalypse also provides us with information about the tribulations of the Churches of Asia. At the time when the apostle was writing his prophecy, the Church of Smyrna was threatened with a severe trial. " I know thy works and tribulation and poverty," John writes, " (but thou art rich), and I know the blasphemy of them which say they are Jews, and are not, but are a synagogue of Satan. Fear none of those things which thou shalt suffer. Behold, the devil is about to cast some of you into prison, that ye may be tried. And ye shall have a tribulation of ten days. Be thou faithful unto death, and I will give thee a crown of life."[2] At Pergamos, Antipas, the faithful witness, had already been killed.[3]

Almost everywhere there had been martyrs; there would certainly be others; and the finer souls were becoming impatient. They asked in anguish when the day of

---

[1] Apoc. i. 9. [2] Apoc. ii. 9-10. [3] Apoc. ii. 13.

triumph would come, and when the Lord was going to revenge those who had given their lives for Him. This is admirably expressed in the vision which follows upon the opening of the fifth seal. " I saw under the altar the souls of them that were slain for the word of God, and for the testimony which they held. And they cried with a loud voice saying: How long, O Lord, holy and true, dost thou not judge and avenge our blood on them that dwell on the earth? And white robes were given unto every one of them, that they should rest yet for a little season, until the time should be fulfilled when their fellow servants and also their brethren were killed, as they were."[1]

The whole Apocalypse breathes an atmosphere of persecution. This unique book was written at a time when the Empire, everywhere, declared its hatred of the Churches and multiplied the number of the martyrs. Many were discouraged. The apostle consoled and fortified them. He put before them the splendour of the triumph that would follow their trial. He did not even shrink from completing the joy of that triumph by the announcement of the fall of the Roman Empire.

" The kings of the earth who have committed fornication and lived deliciously with her shall bewail her, and lament for her, when they shall see the smoke of her burning. Standing afar off for the fear of her torment, saying: Alas! alas! that great city Babylon, that mighty city! For in one hour is thy judgment come.

" And the merchants of the earth shall weep and mourn over her, for no man buyeth their merchandise any more.

" The merchandise of gold and silver, and precious stones, and of pearls, and fine linen, and purple, and silk, and scarlet and thyine wood, and all manner vessels of ivory and all manner vessels of most precious wood, and of brass, and iron, and marble, and cinnamon, and odours,

[1] Apoc. vi. 9-11.

and ointments, and frankincense, and wine, and oil, and fine flour, and wheat, and beasts, and sheep, and horses, and chariots, and bodies and souls of men . . .

"In one hour so great riches is come to nought. . . . Rejoice over her, thou heaven, and ye holy apostles and prophets; for God hath avenged you on her. . . . In her was found the blood of prophets and of saints, and of all that were slain upon the earth."[1]

The prophecy continues at length. The apostle and his readers seem to take pleasure in contrasting the contemporary richness of the accursed city with the ruin into which it would immediately fall. They applauded the fall of the great Babylon, the mother of all vices, who had been so cruel to them. And this attitude is particularly remarkable. The Apocalypse is almost contemporary with the letter of Saint Clement. But Clement admires the Roman Empire; he prays for it and for its leaders; he vaunts its discipline and organization. And in doing so he is maintaining the proud tradition of loyalty inaugurated by Saint Paul. For Saint John, on the contrary, Rome stands out as the city of the demon; it is the irreconcilable enemy of Christ and His saints; and its ruin will mark the beginning of the great triumph reserved for all those who have whitened their robes and have washed them in the blood of the Lamb.

UNDER TRAJAN

The persecution of Domitian was of short duration. The cruel Emperor was the victim of a conspiracy, and his successor, Nerva, withdrew the measures he had taken against all those suspected of living in the Jewish way. The Church began to breathe during the reigns of Nerva and Trajan. This does not mean, of course, that the profession of the Christian was authorized. By the edict of Nero, the simple fact of being a Christian constituted a

[1] Apoc. xviii. 10-17.

capital offence. So that at any moment the faithful and their leaders might expect to be arrested and condemned. If they were not, that was because the local magistrates shut their eyes and showed themselves to be tolerant. An imprudent action on the part of a Christian, an anonymous denunciation, would be likely to awaken their attention and to provoke the right of the law.

The affair of Saint Ignatius of Antioch throws a strong light on the uncertain situation with regard to the Roman State, in which Christianity remained at the beginning of the second century. We are indeed ignorant of the events which led up to the bishop's arrest and condemnation, nor do we know why, instead of undergoing capital punishment at Antioch, he was put aside to be brought to Rome. But it is clear that although the Church of Antioch was profoundly troubled by the imprisonment of its head, it did not itself suffer destruction. The persecution that broke out upon it lasted only a short time; it was already over when Ignatius arrived at Troas; and when the bishop heard the good news he was so encouraged that he asked all the Churches to send delegates, or at least letters, as soon as possible, to the faithful of Syria to congratulate them on their recovery of peace.

Apart from Antioch, the Churches of Asia remained tranquil. Not only did their leaders and faithful not have to suffer, but they were able to manifest freely their respect and admiration for Saint Ignatius. At Philadelphia he received an earnest welcome; he even held discussions with the heretics and encouraged the faithful to unity and concord. At Smyrna, deputations from the Churches of Tralles, Magnesia and Ephesus came to greet him. All this makes it clear that in fact Christianity enjoyed a certain liberty, but that at any moment that liberty ran the risk of being compromised. We must remember also that the communities through which Saint Ignatius journeyed were those in which the Apocalypse had been previously read. During the twelve years which separated the writing of the Apocalypse from the martyrdom of Saint Ignatius, calm had returned to these churches whose anxiety had been described by the apostle. The law had not been modified. A change of Emperor is a sufficient explanation.

The death of Simeon of Jerusalem, which was contemporary with that of Saint Ignatius, seems also to have been an isolated event. In Palestine, the hostility of the Jews and the never-ending disturbances provoked by the Messianic question, added to measures of a general nature, made the situation of the Christians especially precarious. It is not astonishing, therefore, that the Bishop of Jerusalem should have been called to give his witness, at a time when, in general, the peace was not disturbed.

It is probable that Saint Clement of Rome was also put to death in the reign of Trajan. The great bishop is said to have been arrested on the occasion of some sedition among the people and exiled to Chersonesus. His acts, which are obviously legendary, but which may have preserved certain historical traits, add that in this remote country, Clement found two thousand Christians who had long been sentenced to penal servitude. The influence he exercised over them, together with his zeal in preaching the Gospel to the local inhabitants, is said to have drawn the Emperor's attention to him, and by the imperial command he was thrown into the sea with an anchor round his neck.

Here and there, there must have been still other martyrs. We are told, for example, of the names of Terracina, Saint Zoninus of Sozopolis, Saints Zozimus and Rufus of Philippi, and in the course of time the martyrologies became enriched with many legends which refer to Trajan's reign. But on the whole, the Church seems to have enjoyed tranquillity, at least up to the year 112.

Trajan's rescript, discussed above, marks a date in the history of the relations between the Church and the Roman Empire, for it attempted, for the first time, to fix the conditions for the application of the law of Nero. But it was only a compromise; and the rule it formulated was far from being satisfactory to either of the two parties. It is not our own business to indicate its results, for with it this history ends. During the period we have had to survey, the law did not vary; it meant the prohibition of Christianity. The facts, however, were stronger than the prohibition. Christianity never ceased to develop in spite of the laws. It only remains for us to see precisely what was the progress of that expansion.

CHAPTER VII

THE EXPANSION OF CHRISTIANITY

Palestine and Syria. Asia Minor. Macedonia and Greece. Egypt. Edessa.
The West. Social Expansion. Missionary organization.

WHEN in the reign of Nero the two great apostles, Saint Peter and Saint Paul, gave the witness of their blood to Jesus Christ, the Gospel had already been announced in every part of the Roman world and in many places it had crossed the frontier of the Empire. After their death and after the deaths of the other apostles, about whom we have no definite traditions, the expansion of Christianity still went on. We do not know, indeed, who the good workers were. Most often, no doubt, they were simple believers, merchants obliged to travel abroad on business, slaves transported from their native country, soldiers journeying with the legions to which they belonged. Among them also were zealous preachers, prophets or teachers, designated for teaching by a charism, who preached the good news along the great roads to whoever they met on the way. Finally, there must have been the official missionaries, sent by the heads of the great Churches, who followed the example of the apostles and tried to obey the Master's command to preach the Gospel to every creature.

It is not possible for us to mark, even approximately, the progress that was thus accomplished between the death of Nero and the accession of Trajan. The documents are lacking, and they cannot be supplemented by more or less legendary traditions. In any case, even the traditions are

almost silent with regard to these thirty years. Many
Churches glory in having been founded by the apostles.
Very few claim to trace their origin to the time immediately
after the apostles' death.

But at least—and it is indeed something—we can
indicate the conquests effected by Christianity during the
first seventy years of its existence and we can mark out the
boundaries of its expansion at about the year 100.

PALESTINE AND SYRIA

The good news was first preached in Jerusalem, and it
was soon announced throughout the whole of Palestine.
The Acts of the Apostles speak of the evangelization of
Samaria and the plain of Saron; they indicate groups of
believers in Judea and in Galilee, and with more precision
they mention the faithful at Azotus, Lydda, Joppa and
Caesarea. The cities of Ptolemais, Tyre, Sidon, and
Damascus were also reached very rapidly by Christian
propaganda, and it is not impossible that the "Arabia" to
which Saint Paul withdrew after his conversion was simply
the region neighbouring on this last-mentioned city.

Many circumstances, however, ensured that the country
in which Christianity arose should not be that of its full
development. From the beginning the resistance of the
Jews impeded the apostles' preaching. The war which
ended the year 70 with the ruin of Jerusalem considerably weakened the Christian communities in Palestine. It
seems that at the end of the first century the Judaeo-
Christians who had fled to Pella were very few in number,
and that their community, like others that had been able
to maintain themselves here and there in Palestine,
sheltered the last remnants of an exhausted body rather
than the fruitful shoots of a living tree.

Saint Paul and his companions had made Antioch in
Syria the starting point for their missions. It was there
that Christianity was first announced to the pagans; it was

there that the Christians received their name. Saint Peter stayed at Antioch, and it is with his name that the Episcopal role of that city begins. After Evodius, the obscure successor of the prince of the apostles, Saint Ignatius was the third Bishop of Antioch. In his letters he uses the title of Bishop of Syria; but it cannot be definitely determined whether this expression only marks the pre-eminence of Antioch over the other communities of the province, or whether it means that at the beginning of the second century the Church of Antioch alone was regularly organized with its bishop and hierarchy. In any case, at the time when Ignatius was writing his letters, the community of Antioch was numerous; ancient traditions ascribe an apostolic origin to the first Church of the city and trace back the institution of the responsorial chant to Ignatius himself.

ASIA MINOR

We have not the space to give a full account of the spread of the Gospel in Asia Minor. From the time of Saint Paul this vast region had become the chosen land of Christianity. After having preached in Cilicia, the apostle went through the provinces of Lycia, Pamphilia, Pisidia, Lycaonia and Galitia. He made a long stay at Ephesus and presided over the organization of the Christian communities of Colossae, Hierapolis and Laodicea. The first Epistle of Saint Peter, addressed to the elect of the dispersion who were sojourning in Pontus, Galatia, Cappadocia, Asia and Bithynia, witnesses to the importance which these communities had acquired even before the apostle's death. It seems that nowhere was the Gospel more profoundly established at the end of the first century than in the countries of Asia Minor. The apostle Saint John had made Ephesus his home; he addressed the Apocalypse to the Seven Churches of Ephesus, Smyrna, Pergamos, Sardis, Philadelphia, Thyatira and Laodicea. Saint Ignatius of Antioch passed through this region on his way to Rome, and through him we learn of the Churches of Magnesia, Menander and Tralles. It is morally certain that the names that have come down to us are far from being those of all the communities which existed in the time of Trajan. According to Ramsay, the Seven Churches of the Apocalypse each represent a group of Churches, each is a sort of metropolis. They are all placed at the centre of important means of communication, so that the letters sent to them could easily be circulated. Saint Ignatius, on the other hand, says in his last letters that his project of writing to all the Churches could not be carried out owing to his hurried departure from Troas. We do not know what these Churches were, to whom the martyr had no time to write.

The Apocalypse and the letters of Saint Ignatius not only show the existence of many communities in Asia; they also give the impression that these communities contained great numbers of people. The Church of Ephesus was at the head of the Churches of Asia, and Saint Ignatius speaks of the great multitude of its faithful. The Church of Laodicea gloried in its riches.[1] The Church of Smyrna had grown in spite of the persecutions provoked by a powerful Jewish community. And the seer of the Apocalypse, after the hundred and forty-four thousand chosen from all the tribes of Israel have been enumerated, beholds a great multitude which no man could number, of all nations, and kindreds, and people, and tongues. That multitude assuredly existed elsewhere than in his mind. It was the living image of the real Church which never ceased to multiply.

A similar and still more precise impression is afforded by Pliny's letter to Trajan. The governor of Bithynia was literally frightened by the multitude of Christians which he found in the province, and, without doubt, in the neighbouring provinces also. Coming from Rome, where the community was certainly less numerous, he was not

[1] Apoc. iii. 17.

expecting such a sight. "Many persons," he writes, "of all ages and every rank, and even of both sexes, are brought for judgment. The contagion of that superstition has penetrated not the cities only, but the villages and the country. . . . The temples are almost deserted, the solemn sacrifices long disused, the buyers of sacrificial victims almost non-existent." It is possible that Pliny is exaggerating a little in the interests of the cause he is pleading, but the central fact remains certain; at the beginning of the second century Bithynia contained a dense Christian population, and—a remarkable thing—the Gospel had spread even into the country districts. Instead of remaining confined to the cities, it had gained the market-towns and villages. That is the best proof of its influence. Now it must be remembered that Bithynia was not evangelized by Saint Paul, and although its believers are mentioned among those to whom the First Epistle of Saint Peter is addressed, we cannot affirm that the prince of the apostles ever went through it. It is the type of those provinces in which Christianity was announced by unknown missionaries and was propagated in some way by the power of its doctrine alone.

MACEDONIA AND GREECE

We have no precise information, for the period with which we are dealing, about the Churches of Macedonia and Greece which Saint Paul had founded and to which he devoted the best part of his energy. But Saint Polycarp's letter to the Church of Philippi in Macedonia shows that the Christians of that country remained faithful to their traditions. They continued to read the letter which the apostle had sent to them. They welcomed Ignatius and his companions with charity. One of their presbyters, Valens, had indeed not conducted himself irreproachably, but his faults were not of a kind too grave to be pardoned. At Corinth there were more serious disorders; a number of

believers had gone so far as to rebel against their presbyters, and the Church of Rome had been obliged to intervene for the re-establishment of order. It will be remembered that in the time of Saint Paul the faithful at Corinth
had displayed their factious spirit, some claiming to belong
to Saint Paul, others to Apollos, others to Christ. Fifty
years later they were still as undisciplined and had to be
brought back to obedience. But it is remarkable that in
the letter of Saint Clement no mention is made of heresy
among them. Whereas in Asia the preachers of falsehood
succeeded in creating the gravest dangers to Christian
unity, at Corinth it was only the promoters of discord who
disturbed souls.

EGYPT

Of all the eastern regions of the Empire it is Egypt that
has kept most jealously the secret of its Christian origins.
Tradition attributes to Saint Mark, the disciple of Saint
Peter, the foundation of the episcopal see of Alexandria,
and we possess an episcopal roll which does in fact refer
back to him. The Acts of the Apostles, on the other hand,
mentions a Christian called Apollos who came from Alexandria, and the canon of Muratori witnesses to the
existence of an apocryphal letter of Saint Paul to the
Alexandrians. Our positive knowledge stops here. But
the fact that in the reign of Hadrian, the Gnostic Basilides
began his teaching in Egypt is a sure sign that Christianity
had been preached there at a very early date. For the
Gnosticism of Basilides, in spite of some alien elements
mixed up with it, is certainly based on Christianity. It
could not have been preached except by a man who was
familiar with the Gospel teaching. It is also very possible
that some of the most ancient Christian writings were
written in Egypt: an Egyptian origin may reasonably be
attributed to the Epistle to the Hebrews, the Didache, the
letter of Barnabas, the Odes of Solomon, the Preaching of

Peter. To the degree in which any of these attributions is valid it witnesses to the important position taken by Christianity in the region of the Delta.

EDESSA

Before leaving the East, we must cross the frontiers of the Empire. One of the most considerable facts in the history of the expansion of Christianity is the establishment of the Church of Edessa. A tradition collected by Eusebius affirms that the King of Osroene, Abgar the Black, had been in correspondence with Jesus, and that his country had been evangelized by Saint Thomas or Saint Thaddeus. At least as early as the end of the fourth century the tomb of Saint Thomas was venerated at Edessa; and before then, the apocryphal letters from the Saviour to King Abgar were read with respect. Since the entire region of Edessa was full of Christians at the end of the second century, it is at least certain that it had received the good news at a very early date. Still farther East, Arbele and Adiabene were probably reached by the end of the first century. The chronicle of Arbele attributes the evangelization of the country to the apostle Addai, and it gives the names of the bishops who succeeded him, beginning with Pekitha, one of Addai's first converts. The historical value of this chronicle is not above suspicion, but it would be imprudent to deny all value to it, and still more imprudent to contest the fact of the rapid evangelization of the regions of the Euphrates.

THE WEST

In the West the progress of Christianity seems to have been much slower than in the East. The apostles were not so active there, and occasional missionaries were more rare. We know that Saint Peter came to Rome and died there. We know that Saint Paul, brought captive to Rome, stayed

K

there two years, and that later on he was martyred there. It is probable that Saint Paul's disciple Crescentius went into Gaul, and that the great apostle himself carried out his project of going to Spain. We know nothing of the primitive evangelization of the West; our knowledge is indeed very slight.

But the reality was much more considerable. In Italy Saint Paul already encountered Christians at Puteoli;[1] and in the reign of Nero the Roman Church was able to give an "immense multitude" of martyrs. Both Tacitus and Saint Clement use this expression when writing about Nero's persecution, and the agreement between the pagan historian and the Christian writer is significant. No doubt the great trial weakened that Church; but after some years it had regained its strength, and Saint Clement's letter shows it to have been, at the end of the first century, powerful and disciplined, and conscious of being in some way responsible for all the communities. The enthusiastic expressions with which Saint Ignatius greets it, serve to indicate its importance: the Church of Rome is the president of charity. As Saint Denis of Corinth wrote, a little later on, it was customary to show the most active beneficence to all the brethren and to send assistance to the communities of the different towns.

It was in Greek that Clement wrote to the Corinthians. Ignatius wrote in Greek to the Romans. With the exception of Clement, all the first popes bore Greek names. This was because the faithful in Rome, at the end of this first century, were recruited mainly from Greek-speaking circles. No doubt there were among them numerous brethren of Latin origin also. But these formed only a minority. Having come from the East, Christianity long remained in the capital an Oriental thing.

The *Liber Pontificalis* has preserved certain memories of the successors of Saint Peter which perhaps are not wholly legendary. Saint Linus, who is probably mentioned

---

[1] Acts xxviii. 14.

by Saint Paul,[1] is said to have governed the Roman Church for twelve years and to have died a martyr. Saint Cletus or Anacletus is said to have succeeded him as head of the community and to have remained so for about ten years. After him came Saint Clement, whose fame became considerable. "He had known the blessed apostles," writes Saint Irenaeus, "he still had their voice in his ears and their example before his eyes." Saint Evaristus and then Saint Alexander followed Saint Clement in the Apostolic See. Certain liturgical reforms are attributed to them; but they doubtless never even thought of them.

Proconsular Africa was so full of Christians at the end of the second century that Tertullian, not without exaggeration however, could write: "We are men of yesterday; yet we have filled the earth. . . . We could have fought against you even without arms and without rebellion, simply by the civil discord of an unfriendly separation. . . . Without any doubt you would have been terrified in your solitude by the silence of the world and by that kind of deathly torpor into which the entire earth would have fallen."[2] These phrases presuppose that the evangelization of Africa dates back to what was, even then, a remote period; and Carthage must have heard the good news in the time of the apostles. But we know nothing of the life of the African Churches until the year 190, and it is only then that they begin to manifest their vitality.

The same must be said of Gaul, where the Rhone valley gave liberal access to the Christian conquest during the second century; and perhaps of the eastern coasts of Spain also. Unfortunately we cannot rely on the traditions which claim to preserve the memory of Christian origins in these two countries. Even the historical elements that remain in these traditions are too confused to be ascertained with certainty. Besides none of them refer to the period we are studying and so need not be examined here.

The brief indications given above, are almost all that

[1] 2 Timothy iv. 21.   [2] Apolog. xxxvii.

K*

we know about the expansion of Christianity at the end of the first century. But what we know does not correspond to all that happened; far from it. It is certain that many towns, many provinces even, heard the name of Jesus at that period.

It is at this period also that Christianity can be shown to have acquired the sense of its universality. It is Catholic, according to the word which Saint Ignatius brought into his vocabulary and which was to be used to characterize it in the future. The same Saint Ignatius declares that there are bishops throughout the world.[1]

Saint Clement prays that the Creator of the universe "may guard unhurt the number of His elect that has been numbered in all the world."[2]

The author of the Didache expresses himself in a similar way: "As this broken bread was scattered upon the mountains, but was brought together and became one, so let Thy Church be gathered together from the ends of the earth into Thy kingdom. . . . Remember, Lord, Thy Church, to deliver it from all evil and make it perfect in Thy love, and gather it together in its holiness from the four winds, to Thy kingdom which Thou hast prepared for it."[3] The boundaries of the Roman Empire do not come into this reckoning; Christianity has nothing to do with them; the world is its field of action. Even before it has achieved its conquest, almost before it had begun to undertake that conquest, it knows that it must go to the confines of the inhabited world.

SOCIAL EXPANSION

When we gather together the fragments of history that enable us to know the Christianity of about the year 100, what strikes us as much, if not more than its geographical expansion, is its social expansion. Some fifty years before Saint Clement wrote to the Corinthians, Saint Paul had

[1] Ephesians iii.   [2] 1 Clement lix. 2.   [3] Did. ix. 4; x. 5.

said to the faithful of that same Church: " See your calling, brethren; among you there are not many wise men after the flesh, not many mighty, not many noble.   But God hath chosen the foolish things of the world to confound the wise; and God hath chosen the weak things of the world to confound the things which are mighty.   And base things of the world, and things which are despised, hath God chosen, yea, and things which are not, to bring to nought the things that are."[1]   Many other contemporary facts confirm this testimony of the apostle.   At Jerusalem the Church was too poor to cope with all its needs and it had to accept the subsidies generously provided by the other Churches as a sign of recognition towards the most ancient of all the communities.   At Rome the names of the faithful whom Saint Paul greets in the last chapter of his letter, are, for the most part, names of humble folk.   We often come across these names again on inscriptions where they are applied to slaves, freedmen, poor fugitives from the East, with no other civilian status than the name of their native province or that of the master whom they served, and who were lost amid all the chance happenings of the seething life of the capital.

No doubt we must be careful not to exaggerate.   The readers of Saint Paul's Epistles could not have been completely illiterate.   The faithful of Corinth were not so poor as to be unable to send their offerings to Jerusalem, nor those of Philippi as to be incapable of helping Saint Paul with their gifts.   We even know that from the very beginning Christianity was accepted by a certain number of distinguished persons: the proconsul Sergius Paulus at Cyprus, Denis the Areopagite at Athens, Erastus the treasurer at Corinth.   At Thessalonica and Berea several women of high rank were among the converts of Saint Paul.   At Rome, in Nero's reign, Pomponia Graecina was accused of a foreign superstition.   Her husband, as head of the family, claimed the right to judge her and declared her

[1] 1 Cor. i. 26-28.

innocent. It can hardly be doubted that she was a Christian. Believers were to be met with even in the imperial court; for, writing to the Philippians, Saint Paul sends greetings to the saints who are of the household of Caesar: these were probably slaves or freedmen, but perhaps also soldiers. The Epistle to the Romans similarly speaks of Christians who belong to the household of Narcissus and to that of Aristobulus. Narcissus was the freedman and confidant of the Emperor Claudius; Aristobulus was the grandson of Herod the Great. It is clear that the Church drew her recruits from all parts. But on the whole she was still, about the year 70, mainly the refuge of the poor and the humble folk.

Thirty years later that title remained valid. But towards the end of the first century she included an increasingly considerable number of believers of high rank. Pliny the younger attests that in Bithynia there were Christians of all classes; therefore there must have been noble and rich persons among them. Saint Ignatius of Antioch, writing to the Romans, begs them not to oppose his martyrdom; he must therefore have thought that there were believers in the Roman community of sufficient influence to obtain his pardon. He gives to the Church of Rome the glorious title of the president of charity; and from this we may conclude to the liberality of that Church with regard to the faithful throughout the entire world. In Domitian's reign, the consul Titus Flavius Clement and his wife Domitilla were Christians; they were closely related to the Emperor. The consul Acilius Glabrio was also a Christian. There were or had been Christians in the noble family of the Acilii. And these rich converts showed their generosity by giving property to the Church to be used as burying grounds for their brethren. The cemetery of Domitilla on the Via Ardeatina opened out into land which belonged to the wife of the Consul Clement; that of Priscilla, on the Salarian way, was installed in the property of the Acilii. The correspondence between Seneca and Saint Paul is apocryphal, but there were Christians in the *gens Annaea,* though at what precise date it is difficult to ascertain. At Smyrna, in the time of Saint Ignatius, Gabia, the wife of the procurator, was converted.

The number of Christians in the imperial court increased also. It is probable that Clement was a freedman of Domitilla and her family. The two believers whom he charges to take his letter to Corinth, Claudius Ephebus and Valerino Vito, seem to have belonged to the Emperor's household. These are only a few facts which have come down to us by chance. They enable us to conclude that the social ascent of Christianity, which had begun from its earliest days, was rapidly developing about the year 100.

MISSIONARY ORGANIZATION

The two facts which most strike us when studying the history of the Church at the end of the first century, are its geographical expansion and its numerical increase. But they are not the only ones. We are bound to ask, for example, how the Christian conquest was organized and what methods were used to turn its success to account. On this subject P. Batiffol writes: "It is remarkable that the propagation of Christianity was not the work of missionaries. Saint Paul, bringing the Gospel to Cyprus, Galatia, Macedonia, Achaia, perhaps to Spain, is the missionary *par excellence*; but he was to have no imitators in the generations which followed on that of the apostles. The successors of the apostles were not missionaries but bishops. In that period Christianity obscurely won its way by degrees; it advanced step by step along the great Roman roads. The evangelization of Africa, for example, has no history; neither has that of Britain. "As much might be said of almost every part of the Christian world; and it is an astonishing fact. It is true that other religious movements, more or less contemporary with Christianity, spread in an analogous way. We do not know any more about the propagandists of Isis or the missionaries of Mithra than we do about the preachers of Christianity. The Oriental cults were gradually introduced into the Empire by soldiers' merchants, slaves and travellers, and it was by chance encounters that they first recruited their believers. We need not be astonished that Providence used similar means to make Christianity known to the world.

But the resemblances should not be over-stressed. Much more than, and in a very different way from the Oriental religions, Christianity was a doctrine. It affirmed itself as an orthodoxy and dreaded nothing so much as heresy. Now this doctrine was found identically the same from one end of the world to the other. Those who preached it were not prophets or inspired persons, but witnesses to tradition. The Church, indeed, respectful of the rights of God, never claimed to extinguish or grieve the spirit; it recognized legitimate prophecy; it allowed the charismatics to speak in the assemblies. But from the time of the apostles, and still more after their death, it claimed a sovereign right of control over the manifestations attributed to the Holy Ghost. The letter of Saint Clement is the most characteristic witness to that attitude; everything in it is calm, measured, reasonable; everything has the mark of ecclesiastical order. The authorized spokesman of the Roman Church has about him nothing of the enthusiast. Saint Ignatius of Antioch has a very different manner. He is much more personal, much more emotional also than Saint Clement. The Epistle to the Romans in particular is made up of mystic rhapsodies. Nevertheless one should not allow oneself to be deceived by appearances. This impassioned writer is the most definite preacher of the episcopate and of obedience. Thus individual differences are effaced before doctrinal unity.

The tradition to which all remained faithful was that of the apostles. These were only recently departed, and

Saint John was still continuing at Ephesus his long career when Saint Clement wrote to the Corinthians. We know little with certainty about their preaching, their activity, their death. But their authority is beyond discussion. "The apostles," Clement declares, "were sent to us as messengers of the good news by the Lord Jesus Christ. Jesus Christ was sent by God. The Christ therefore is from God and the apostles from Christ: both these things follow in good order from the will of God. Having therefore received their instructions from our Lord Jesus Christ, and being fully convinced by His resurrection, the apostles, confirmed by the word of God, went forth in the assurance of the Holy Spirit preaching the good news that the Kingdom of God is coming. They preached from district to district, and from city to city, and they appointed their first converts, testing them by the Spirit, to be bishops and deacons of the future believers."[1] The bishops, chosen by the apostles, received successors in their turn; and thus the tradition was faithfully conserved. Saint Ignatius was no less faithful in bringing out the authority of the apostles. "Be diligent therefore," he writes to the Magnesians, "to be confirmed in the ordinances of the Lord and the apostles."[2] Thus in his eyes, the apostles have the same power, the same value as the Lord. As for himself, he is only a poor convict. "I did not think myself competent, as a convict," he declares to the Trallians, "to give you orders like an apostle."[3] He apologizes when writing to the Romans: I do not give you orders as did Peter and Paul: they were apostles.[4] They had a privileged and incommunicable authority; that authority still belonged to the decisions they had made and to the letters they had written under the inspiration of the Holy Spirit.

The Didache expresses this truth in its very title: it is the doctrine of the Lord taught to men by the twelve

[1] 1 Clem. xcii. 1-4.   [2] Magn. xiii. 1.
[3] Trall. iii. 3.   [4] Rom. iv. 3.

apostles. What the Lord preached, the apostles have repeated throughout the whole world; and this is what must be believed. There were to be numerous writings later on with analogous titles: the Didascalia of the Apostles, the Apostolical Tradition, the Apostolical Constitutions. All of them were only expressions of the same idea which had already been put forward with incomparable force at the end of the first century.

Fidelity to the apostolic tradition ensured unity of doctrine. " If one tried to draw the religious map of the ancient world," writes P. Batiffol, " in so far as that is possible, and in the way it has already been done for certain provinces, such as Asia, it would be full of the most decided contrasts. In the pagan religions, regional differences are a normal feature; and this is also strongly marked in Gnosticism. It is easy to distinguish at once Syrian Gnosticism from that of Alexandria, Asiatic Gnosticism from Roman. In fact Gnosticism is a good example of a perpetually changing syncretism, assimilating different elements according to the regions in which it was propagated and the men who taught it. . . . Catholicism, on the contrary, stands out as endowed with an astounding homogeneity. It was not, like Mithraism, the religion of a particular class, since it was propagated among all classes, from the slave Onesimus to the consul Flavius Clement. In truth, its members were mainly ordinary and unlettered people, the *tenuiores* and *simpliciores*. In a province such as Bithynia, the cultured Pliny only saw in these converts of every rank and age and of both sexes, a debased superstition carried to great lengths. This is how it must have appeared everywhere to men of biased minds like that of Pliny. The astonishing thing is that, penetrating so deeply into the soul of the pagan masses, Christianity did not become corrupted by syncretizing itself with all the errors that are, for example, denounced in the Epistle to the Colossians or in the message to the Seven Churches in the Apocalypse."

The fact is that Catholicism kept its faith; it maintained it from one end of the world to the other. Saint Ignatius was governing the Church of Antioch when he was arrested in order to be taken to Rome. We know nothing about his origins or his formation. But it has been remarked that many traits in his thought and style remind one of Saint John. This does not mean that he was taught by the apostle. But it shows at least that the Johannine thought and style were not the exclusive property of the author of the fourth Gospel. In every place through which the glorious martyr passed he was received by the communities; and the Churches whom he did not visit sent deputations to greet him. He was not personally known; he was recognized as a witness of Christ and a guardian of orthodoxy—that was his importance. Everywhere, or almost everywhere in Asia, the heretics were active and were attempting to divide the Body of Christ. Ignatius did not communicate with them. By what sign did he recognize them, except by the novelty of their doctrine and their independence with regard to the established authorities? He put the faithful on guard against their errors. Submission to the bishop, to the presbyterium and to the deacons is the best guarantee of truth. When he arrived at Smyrna he sent a letter to the distant Church of the Romans. He knew that that Church had the same faith and hope as himself. He was certain that his Epistle would be received by the brethren. Thus from East to West there flowed one single current of life.

In certain ways the Christian dispersion may be compared to that of the Jews. In both cases there was the same fidelity to traditions and the same concern for orthodoxy. But on their side the Jews had the antiquity of their traditions, the small number of pagans whom they would allow into their communities, and above all their sacred books. They formed a race apart; they constituted a nation, even after the ruin of Jerusalem: with them, converts were never more than a minority, and before they

were received they had to give many proofs of their
fidelity. The Christians, on the contrary, were only of
yesterday. If they presented themselves, and with justice,
as the continuers and heirs of the Jewish traditions, they
had to prove their claims; and that proof was made all the
less easy from the fact that it demanded an allegorical
interpretation of the Law. They gave a liberal welcome
to the pagans who came to them, without demanding anything except faith in Jesus Christ and conversion of life.
And this multitude of men and women who came from
everywhere, who had previously professed the most diverse
belief and practised the most different religions, they
assimilated without difficulty. Far from being corrupted
by the ingress of the pagans, Christianity, while keeping
its own identity intact, purified them. Those who more
or less refused to accept the whole of its dogma and the
whole of its morality, it repulsed. Those were the
heretics.

Those Christians, however, did not yet possess a
definite canon of the sacred books which were proper to
them. At the end of the first century this canon was in
process of formation, and we could point out in the writing of Saint Clement, Saint Ignatius, in the Didache and
elsewhere, unequivocal traces of the use of the Gospels and
Epistles, quoted as inspired Scripture. But we should be
obliged to indicate at the same time the loose way in which
most of these quotations are made and also the utilization
of texts that were not destined to enter the canon. In
short, we may say that the Apostolic Fathers knew the
Gospel accounts, the letters of Saint Paul, etc., but they
had not yet come to feel for them that exclusive respect
which the Jews had towards their sacred books. It is therefore all the more remarkable that they accepted hardly any
of those legendary elements which the writers of apocrypha
were to multiply in the succeeding generations. The un-
written words of the Lord, the *agrapha*, which they mention, have, as a rule, a genuine sound, and may have been

transmitted by oral tradition.   Even when they utilize, as
Saint Ignatius may have done, apocryphal writings such as
the Gospel of Peter, they do so only in passing and without
giving more credit to these books than they deserve.   On
any hypothesis, Scripture had for them only an accessory
part to play; it was upon tradition that they depended; and
each of them could have made the words of Papias his own:
" I did not think that the things that could be drawn from
books would be as useful to me as those which come from
the living and abiding word."

Once again we find ourselves brought back to tradition.
In this period at the end of the first century, it is that
which explains and illuminates everything.   The Christian
was then what he has remained ever since, the man of
tradition.   The extraordinary thing is that that tradition
has been maintained in its integrity in spite of the almost
paradoxical richness of its content.

This has often astonished the historians; but perhaps
none of them have said so with so much energy as Harnack,
in a famous passage that deserves frequent perusal.
" When Christianity first appeared on pagan soil, it was
rich with a plenitude that embraced within its unity the
most well marked differentiations.   Each of its elements
seemed to be the principal, if not the only one.   Christianity is the preaching of God the Father Almighty, of His
Son Jesus Christ, the Lord, and of the Resurrection.   It is
the Gospel of the Saviour and of salvation, of the redemption and the new creation.   It is the herald of man's divin-
ization.   It is the Gospel of love and brotherly assistance.
It is the religion of the Spirit and of strength, of moral
seriousness and holiness.   It is the religion of authority
and of absolute faith, and it is also the religion of reason
and of clear knowledge; and it is again a religion of mysteries.   It is the message of the birth of an entirely new
people who, nevertheless, secretly pre-existed from the
beginning of things.   It is the religion of a holy book.
Everything which can be called religion, it possesses.

Everything which can be conceived of as religion, it is. It is syncretism, but a syncretism of a particular kind; it is the syncretism of the universal religion. It established itself thanks to the employment of every religious force and every religious form; it took them all into its service. How poor, necessitous and limited are the other religions in relation to it. It is impossible to embrace this unique religion with one glance; nevertheless a single name embraces it and sums it up, that of Jesus Christ."

This is indeed the unforgettable and moving spectacle that the Church at the end of the first century presents to one who has tried as well as possible to recall some of the most decisive years of its history, those during which the last apostles died and their first successors began to carry on their task.

Saint Paul had already written: " I determined not to know anything among you, save Jesus Christ, and him crucified."[1] Saint Ignatius of Antioch echoes these words: " May no creature, visible or invisible, seek to stay my possession of Jesus Christ! Let there come on me fire, and cross, and struggles with wild beasts, cutting, and tearing asunder, rackings of bones, mangling of limbs, crushing of my whole body, cruel tortures of the devil, may I but attain to Jesus Christ! What would the possession of the earth and of the kingdoms of this world profit me? It is much more glorious for me to die in Christ Jesus than to reign over the ends of the earth. I seek Him who died for our sake. I desire Him who rose again for us."[2]

Many centuries have passed since Saint Ignatius wrote these admirable words. Christianity is always living. To those who look at it from outside and do not know the fullness of its life from experience, it may often seem that it is dead or about to die after having been completely transformed. Those who live by it and who daily experience its inexhaustible fecundity know well that it is, now

[1] 1 Cor. ii. 2.   [2] Rom. v. 3-vi. 1.

as of old, the hidden treasure and the precious pearl. One name sums up what it is for us, what it was for those saints of old whose lives have sometimes lit up the aridity of these pages: Jesus Christ who was yesterday, who is to-day, and who will be for ever.

BIBLIOGRAPHY

WE shall confine ourselves to indicating a few works that are particularly important or easily accessible. But in the spirit of this series we shall not attempt an exhaustive bibliography, which in any case would not befit the elementary character of this book.

We presuppose that everyone knows and possesses the following essential books:

ON CHRISTIAN LITERATURE

A. PUECH. *Histoire de la littérature grecque chrétienne*. Vols. 1-2. Paris. 1928.

P. DE LABRIOLLE. *Histoire de la littérature latine chrétienne*. Paris. 1920.

O. BROADENHEWER. *Geschichte der altkirchen Literatur*. Vol. 1. 2nd edition. Fribourg. 1913.

J. TIXERONT. *Précis de Patrologie*. Paris. 1918. English edition: *History of Dogma*.

G. RAUSCHEN. *Patrologie*. 10th edition. Fribourg. 1931.

ON CHRISTIAN DOCTRINE

J. LEBRETON. *Histoire du dogme de la Trinité*. Vol. 1. 6th edition. Paris. 1928. Vol. 2. Paris. 1928.

ON THE CHURCH

P. BATIFFOL. *L'Eglise naissante et la catholicisme*. Paris. 1909. English edition: *Primitive Catholicism*. Longmans, Green & Co. 1911.

ON THE EXPANSION OF CHRISTIANITY

A. VON HARNACK. *Die Mission und Auslreitung des Christentums in der ersten drei Jahrunderten*. 4th edition. Leipzig. 1924.

CHAPTER I. THE WRITINGS

M. G. LAGRANGE. *L'Evangile selon S. Jean.* Paris. 1925.
E. B. ALLO. *L'Apocalypse.* Paris. 1921.
LIGHTFOOT. *The Apostolic Fathers.* 1889.
H. HEMMER. *Clement de Rome.* Paris. 1909.
H. HEMMER. *La doctrine des apôtres et la lettre de Barnabe.* Paris. 1909.
A. LELONG. *Saint Ignace d'Antioche.* Paris. 1910.
A. AMANN. Article: " Apocryphes du Nouveau Testament " in the *Supplement du Dictionnaire de la Bible,* vol. 1.
J. M. LAGRANGE. " L'Evangile selon les Hébreux " in the *Revue Biblique.* 1922.
P. VAGANAY. *L'Evangile de Pierre.* Paris. 1930.
P. BATIFFOL and J. LABOURT. *Les Odes de Solomon.* Paris. 1910.

CHAPTER II. CHRISTIAN LIFE

DOM CABROL. *La Prière des premiers chrétiens.* Paris. 1928.
J. COPPENS. *L'Imposition des mains et rites connexes dans le Nouveau Testament et dans l'ancienne Eglise.* Paris and Louvain. 1925.
P. BATIFFOL. *L'Eucharistie.* 7th edition. Paris. 1920.
W. GOOSENS. *Les origines de l'Eucharistie, sacrament et sacrifice.* Paris. 1931.
H. LEITZMANN. *Messe und Herrenmahl. Eine Studie zur Geschichte der Liturgie.* Bonn. 1926.
F. J. DOLGER.
B. CAPELLE. *Les Origines du symbole romain, in Recherches de théologie ancienne et médiévale.* 1930.
J. DE GHELLINCK. *L'Histoire du symbole des apôtres, in Recherches de Science religieuse.* 1928.

CHAPTER III. THE CHURCH AND THE CHURCHES

H. DE GENOUILLAC. *L'Eglise chrétienne au temps de S. Ignace.* Paris. 1907.
A. MICHELS. *L'Origine de l'épiscopat.* Louvain. 1900.
H. B. SWETE. *Essays on the Early History of the Church and Ministry.* 1918. (Anglican tendency.)
J. TIXERONT. *La Théologie ante-Nicenne.* 9th edition. Paris. 1924. pp. 131-142.
P. MEDEBIELLE. Article: " Apostolat " in the *Supplement du Dictionnaire de la Bible,* vol. 1.
H. WEINEL. *Die Wirungen des Geistes und der Geister in nachapostolichen Zeitalter.* Fribourg. 1899. (Protestant.)
R. KNOPF. *Nach Apostolischer Zeilalter.* Tubingen. 1905. (Protestant.)
DOM CHAPMAN. " La chronologie des premières listes épiscopales de Rome " in the *Revue Bénédictine.* 1901-2.
J. GASQUET. " S. Ignatius and the Roman Primacy " in *Studies.* 1904.

CHAPTER IV. THE JUDAEO-CHRISTIANS

M. J. LAGRANGE. *Le Messianisme chez les Juifs.* Paris. 1909.
G. HOENNICKE. *Das Judencristentum im 1 und 2 Jahrhundert.* Berlin. 1908.
O. CULLMANN. *Le problème littéraire et historique du roman pseudo-Clementine.* Paris. 1930.
H. WAITZ. *Die Pseudo-Klementinen Homilien und Recognitionen.* Leipzig. 1904.
W. BRANDT. *Elchasai, Ein Religionstifter und sein Werk.* Leipzig. 1912.
M. J. LAGRANGE. " La Gnose Maudeen et la tradition évangélique " in *Revue Biblique.* 1927. 1928.

CHAPTER V. HERESY

L. GERFAUX. " La Gnose simonienne " in *Recherches des Sciences Religieuses.* 1925. 1926.
L. GERFAUX. " La vrai prophétie des Clementines " in *Recherches des Sciences Religieuses.* 1928.
G. BARDY. " Cerinthe " in *Revue Biblique.* 1922.
Z. DE FAYE. *Gnostiques et gnosticisme. Etude critique des documents du gnosticisme chrétien aux 2 et 3ieme siècles.* 2nd edition. Paris. 1925.

CHAPTER VI. CHRISTIANITY AND THE EMPIRE

C. CALLEWAERT. Articles on " Les origines de la legislation persécutrice " in *Revue d'histoire ecclésiastique.* 1901-2-11. *Revue des Questions historiques.* 1903-4-5-7.
P. ALLARD. *Le Christianism et l'empire romain.* Paris. 1897.
R. SALEILLES. " L'organisation juridique des premières communicantes " in *Mélanges.* P. Girard. 1912.

CHAPTER VII. CHRISTIAN EXPANSION

J. RIVIERE. *La propagation du christianisme dans les trois premiers siècles.* Paris. 1907.
H. LECLERCQ. Article: " Expansion du Christianisme " in *Diction d'archéol. chret. et de liturgie.*